Good Lord, Why Not?

THELMA HARPER

as told to

VICKI LAWRENCE *and* MONTY AIDEM

THOMAS NELSON
Since 1798

NASHVILLE   DALLAS   MEXICO CITY   RIO DE JANEIRO   BEIJING

Published in Nashville, Tennessee, by Thomas Nelson. Thomas Nelson is a registered trademark of Thomas Nelson, Inc.

Thomas Nelson, Inc., titles may be purchased in bulk for educational, business, fund-raising, or sales promotional use. For information, please e-mail SpecialMarkets@ThomasNelson.com.

Library of Congress Cataloging-in-Publication Data

Harper, Thelma.
    Mama for president : good Lord, why not? / Thelma Harper.
      p. cm.
    ISBN 978-1-4016-0409-7
    1. Presidents—United States—Election—Humor. 2. United States—Politics and government—Humor. 3. American wit and humor. I. Title.
PN6231.P693H37 2008
818'.602—dc22   2008005528

Printed in the United States of America

08 09 10 11 12 RRD 5 4 3 2 1

Contents

☆ Contents ☆

Introduction: Why Me?

*L*isten up, America! The solution to all your problems has just plopped right in your lap. It's Mama for president! That's right, yours truly, Mama Thelma Harper, at your service. I say if you want it done right, get a woman to do it. If Hillary can go as far as she has gone, I can go even farther. Many women have made names for themselves in politics, so why not me? India was run by Indira Gandhi, England had Margaret Snatcher, and you'll all remember that Perón lady in South America, who ran her country and still had time to sing on Broadway. Her theme song, "Don't Cry for Me, Art and Tina," has always been one of my favorites. And let's not forget Janet Reno, who was America's attorney general. Janet was all business, not into style or fashion. Hell, J. Edgar Hoover looked better in a gown than she did. But old Janet got the job done. She was a no-nonsense gal who you had to listen to because she was smart, dedicated, and because you knew she could beat the crap out of you. I'm a no-nonsense gal in the Janet Reno mold, although the Good Lord was nice enough to send a little more estrogen my way.

So why can't I stick *my* butt in the seat of government? I merely plan to take my rightful place in political history, alongside other semi-intelligent people.

You've been hearing a lot of politicians like Mr. Barack Obama talk about "change." Well, I know a lot about that. I've been through the change, and take it from me—it's not all it's cracked up to be.

I will be the first candidate who can give you commonsense advice based on my many years of experience. I have been on this earth for quite a while, and I'm not ashamed to admit it. In fact, I've been around so long, I remember when Bob Barker wore a fur parka. In fact, the only person I can think of that's older than me, right off the top of my head, is John McCain. And there's nothing wrong with getting old. With age comes wisdom, not to mention incontinence. So listen to my advice, and you'll be better off. I realize the road ahead could be rough, but I know a lot about roughage. And yes, I may be old, but I'm as perky as Kelly Ripa with a double espresso. In fact, as I write this book to officially launch my campaign, I'm so filled with anticipation and excitement, I'm tingling. It must be the excitement of the coming campaign, although it could be from that breakfast burrito I had this morning.

I've always been a curious and inquisitive person. I wonder about many things and want answers. In addition to the major issues of our times, I want answers to the things we all wonder about, like, how do blind dogs get around? . . . Who did the *Elephant Man* make fun of? . . . and if Lindsay Wagner is getting such a good night's rest on her Sleep Number bed, how come she always sounds so depressed?

I believe you want your president to be a thoughtful, reflective individual, so I will share with you some of my most reflective thoughts. And in that vein, I have put a lot of quiet thought and reflection into a recurring feature for this book, which is "People Who Should Be Tasered"—folks who are standing in our way and holding us back—like the inventor of fingerless gloves. If a glove has no fingers, what the devil do I need gloves for?

Along with my list of people who should be Tasered, you will also find some of my most profound quotations, my best commonsense answers to your questions, and some questions the other candidates aren't asking.

I have many ideas to improve America, some of which are legal. And I will put forth all of my ideas in this book. Your job is to buy it. So if you're thumbing through this book in a bookstore or book department, how about coughing up a few bucks? This ain't a library!

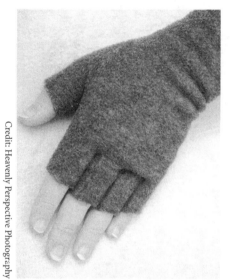

Credit: Heavenly Perspective Photography

A Fingerless Glove

And now, as you make your way to the cash register, let's begin our discussion of my strategy, my position on the issues, and my plan for America so together we can work toward the happy day when I bring my box of Fiber One onto *Air Force One.*

My Campaign

I will run a clean campaign and try not to reveal any of the dirty little secrets all of my opponents are hiding. I will choose instead to inspire Americans with my common sense, strong moral character, and the kind of intelligence the *TV Guide* crossword puzzle is no match for. I will not be a slave to any special-interest groups, although I should disclose that I am a lifelong member of the Tony Orlando fan club.

My record is pretty clean, except for one isolated incident in which I may have bent the rules of the state of Missouri a little bit in order to get out of a bad time-share deal in Branson.

I am family oriented, and I have worked hard to raise a family, especially considering what a stupid moron my son is.

You will never see me removing any dentures in public, and I have been told that I perform very few involuntary bodily functions for a person my age. And most important, my fellow Americans, I'm proud to say that there are no skeletons in my closet; just some mousetraps and a roach motel with no vacancies.

I am willing to debate my opponents any time, any where. You can count on me to show those bozos how mixed up they are, which

I will try to do without cussing too much. There is no reason to use salty language, even if the other candidates are clueless. In any event, those competitors better think twice if they think I'm a newcomer to making an argument. As an old woman with a lot of time on my hands, arguing with people is my main activity. But I should warn you that I have been known to have a bit of a temper. In spite of that, I will try to hold back before things get physical. The last thing this country needs is to see the potential leaders of the free world rolling around on the floor live on CNN. And I won't impose any ground rules for our debates except for a glass of bicarbonate on my desk and two or three emergency bathroom breaks if needed. When it comes to debating our nation's most pressing issues, I have answers for questions no one's even thought of. So tell Anderson Cooper, Wolf Blister, and all the others to fire away!

It costs a lot of money to run a campaign, but I am up to the challenge. I have several bake sales planned, not to mention a $5-per-plate fund-raising dinner at the Elks Club (dessert extra). You may also receive a phone call asking for donations from a "Mama for President" campaign volunteer, as soon as I get one. If you get called, please don't hang up until the volunteer is finished begging. Regarding all contributions to my campaign, you may be certain that none of your funds will be used for personal purposes, unless I run out of Maalox while on the campaign trail. I want to issue a warning to all contributors: If your check bounces, I have an arrangement for it to be taped on the wall at the Dollar Store for all to see. I will also accept lottery tickets, but don't come crying to me if there's a $100 winner in there. Even nonfinancial contributions will be welcome, and if you are so inclined, I'm a size 16. Furthermore, I believe in putting my money where my mouth is, so I will follow in the footsteps of that Mick Romney guy and spend some of my own funds on my campaign.

As for selling my message, I know I will need a slogan to capture the imagination of the voters and separate me from the other, less interesting wanna-bes. Over the years, presidential candidates have come up with catchy slogans, like Herbert Hoover's "a chicken in every pot," Dwight Eisenhower's "I like Ike," and Richard Nixon's "Nixon's the One." (Yes, "Nixon's the One." And according to the Watergate investigation, it turns out he was.) Well, I, too, have been working on slogans to bring my message to the people. Some of the slogans I have been considering are: *A full-figured woman whose time has come; An old broad for a new day; A simple*

Credit: William Wade

mind for a complex time; A hot flash forward; and *Add some gray to the red, white, and blue.*

Trustworthy

Credit: William Wade

Credit: William Wade

Compassionate

Tough

Credit: William Wade

Education

I will make education a priority in my administration because an educated public will not be so irritating. Right now, there are many annoying people we have to put up with, and I'm sure you know what I'm talking about. For example, cashiers. Why do they ask you such stupid questions?

I was at a leading discount store the other day. I bought Pepto Bismol, Ex-lax, and toilet paper. And the cashier said, "Do you want a gift receipt with that?"

I said, "Yeah, I'm going to give all this stuff to my best friend because she's expecting a bowel movement any day now!" What kind of bimbo thinks you're going to give Ex-lax as a gift? Talk about the gift that keeps on giving!

And as long as we're talking about the stupid, how about those stories we've all heard, about women who gave birth and never knew they

were pregnant. Good Lord! I mean, your ankles are swollen, your boobs are killing you, and you're throwing up every morning. You're either pregnant, or the devil's taken over your body. Get some help before your head starts spinning around!

Credit: William Wade

One woman who didn't know she was pregnant said she just thought her stomach was giving her trouble. Let me just say this: I ate a bad tostada once. It burned, it throbbed, and it tingled. But if at some point, it had started to *kick* . . . I think I would have gone for help.

By the way, I have a proposal for our schools that will be of great benefit to our children. If elected, I will make it illegal for a high school cafeteria worker to work without a hairnet on her head *and* her arms.

Of course, education doesn't only take place in schools. I have found education on a variety of subjects in places like the popular women's magazines. They always have interesting quizzes, facts, and tidbits. For example, the other day, I read an interesting article in one of the leading women's magazines that said a sneeze is the closest thing to an orgasm. That's right; a sneeze is the closest thing to an orgasm. Well, if you think about it, there are some similarities. You close your eyes . . . you make a funny little noise . . . and I personally have been known to say, "God bless you" after both of them.

Think of the positive impact that better education will have on our lives. For example, an educated public will not spend its money on something like "potpourri." It's a bag of twigs and dirt, for heaven's sake! For $49.95! And some people give it as a gift! When I'm president, it will be illegal to give such stupid gifts.

And speaking of stupid gifts, what kind of man needs a motorized tie rack? I mean, how lazy are you if you need help moving ties?

In my life, I have found that in addition to education, there is the importance of common sense, which comes into play in everyday life. For example, if someone calls at one o'clock in the morning and asks what you're wearing, common sense tells you he's probably not with the Census Bureau.

Throughout this book, I will offer answers to commonsense questions you have raised.

Commonsense Answers from Your Candidate

THE QUESTION: What's the best way to end a boring conversation?

MY ANSWER: Pay for the haircut and leave.

UNDERSTANDING OTHER CULTURES

*A*s a presidential candidate, I realize it is important to understand the cultures of people who live in other countries. Many of them are just like us. For example, I have a lot of respect for our neighbors to the north, in Canada. I have always thought of Canadians as Americans with warmer jackets.

We must be tolerant and respectful of all cultures, no matter how weird and disgusting they are. The other day, I saw a special on the National Geographic Channel with a tribe of people running around buck naked. I came away from that experience with the wonderful insight that stretch marks have no borders. You know, those women had never, ever worn a bra! If they ever do, Grandma will need a 44 Long.

FOREIGN INFLUENCES IN AMERICA

Now that there are so many Spanish-speaking people in our country, you and I may hear Spanish phrases and not understand them. But Spanish is really a pretty easy language. For example, take the phrase *la bamba*. That is Spanish for "the bamba."

I have actually considered learning more Spanish—if not the whole language, then maybe just enough to ask the busboy at the Mexican restaurant why the plate is so darn hot. And speaking of food . . .

Many foods of foreign cultures have been brought to our country, although I'm wondering how many of these foods are for real. For example, I would bet no one in Japan actually eats raw fish. It was probably a little joke played on Americans for winning World War II.

Still, every time I enjoy exotic delicacies like Italian sausage, Polish kielbasa, or German knucklewurst, I'm thankful foreigners have come to America and brought their wieners with them.

I like to think of myself as an expert on foreign relations, thanks to the many hours I have spent watching the Travel Channel. I have learned about the different ways foreigners work, relax, and gratify themselves. So consider me your foreign-relations candidate and know that I will make sure that many Americans have relations with foreigners.

THE UN

And now to an important subject regarding foreign relations. My fellow Americans, I'm sick and tired of the UN being on U.S. soil and supported by U.S. taxpayers. When I am president, in order to save money, the UN will be disbanded, and all disputes between nations will be settled at the International House of Pancakes. This will not only be sensible but practical, because everyone knows that IHOP is pretty much empty after breakfast. Besides, I think if I were to sit down over some silver dollar pancakes with that little guy in North Korea, he'd be disarming his weapons before you can say, "Rooty Tooty Fresh 'N Fruity." (That is not a personal comment on the leader of North Korea. It is my favorite dish at IHOP.) By the way, I believe that North Korea's dictator is secretly a great admirer of American entertainment. As proof, look how he has styled his hair like a famous American TV Star.

A coincidence? I don't think so. By the way, Kim is also probably not very funny in a nightclub.

The IHOP: the new venue for working on foreign relations.

Credit: AP Photos

Credit: AP Photos

Promoting America

We are a country of many beautiful regions across a vast expanse, from the purple mountains' majesty to those amber waves of bran. As your president, I will promote our fine country and encourage tourism here. We have so many wonderful tourist spots, some natural and some unnatural, like the Grand Canyon, New York's Times Square, and Seattle's Space Noodle. And let's not forget Las Vegas. I love going to Las Vegas. The last time there, I was quite taken by the Paris casino and its Eiffel Tower. It was beautiful. And I understand there's one just like it in France. Isn't that just like the French to horn in on our great ideas? By the way, this may surprise you, but I have actually visited France. While there, I saw the *Mona Lisa*. It was the only thing in France that smiled at me.

Mostly, I confine my travels to fine American destinations where there's friendly hospitality and food that's easy to chew. If it's chopped, mashed, or puréed, warm up some for me. But watch the spices. When you're my age, you have to be pretty darn careful. You've heard

Credit: BigStockPhoto

of eating something that didn't agree with you? On my last vacation, I ate something that didn't even want to hear my side of the story!

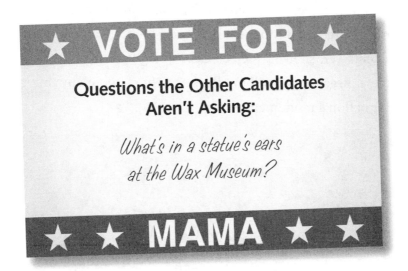

★ **VOTE FOR** ★

Questions the Other Candidates Aren't Asking:

What's in a statue's ears at the Wax Museum?

★ ★ **MAMA** ★ ★

I, for one, love visiting Florida, where many senior citizens live. And why not? It's a geriatric paradise. The weather is pleasant, there are lots of pharmacies, and each day at twilight you can look around and see old couples stop their bickering, look into each other's eyes, and whisper those three magic words: *early bird dinner.*

As president, I will encourage people to visit our nation's capital—which I will probably keep in Washington DC—where you'll find many of our most famous landmarks, like the Washington Monument, the Capitol, and the Lincoln Memorial, which I visited recently for inspiration. It was on that spot that I knew my destiny lay ahead as a presidential candidate. As I looked up into the great emancipator's nostrils, I felt his spirit telling me to go out there and bring our people together, unify our country, and avoid the theater.

And let's not forget that beautiful monument to some of our presidents, called Mount Rushmore, in South Dakota. And do you want to hear something interesting? I read that some guy has a job filling the cracks on Mount Rushmore. I didn't realize any of the presidents were showing their cracks. I thought it was just their faces up there. Regardless, I will put the same effort into maintaining all of our national monuments.

Commonsense Answers
from Your Candidate

THE QUESTION: As a proud Irish-American, I would like to know: Would you kiss the Blarney Stone?

MY ANSWER: Yes, but that's as far as I'd go.

The Military

As my first military priority, I will send troops into the country of Myanmar, and they will remain there until the Myanmartians do the proper thing. I'm referring, of course, to that name change they tried to sneak past us a while back, when they changed the name of the place from Burma to Myanmar. What a shifty move *that* was! I bought a nice green globe of the world in 1958, and I'll be darned if I'm going to take a magic marker and start crossing out the lettering. What the hell is going on over there? The only reason to change your name is if you get married or you owe a

Commonsense Answers
from Your Candidate

THE QUESTION: Is it safe
to visit Tijuana?

MY ANSWER: Yes, if
you're a germ.

lot of money. They've got a lot of nerve trying to pull a fast one on us, not to mention the fact that they have ruined the market for Burma Shave! So, Myanmar, you're on notice. And, Siam, you're NEXT!

DON'T ASK/DON'T TELL

I have heard about a policy in the military called, "Don't ask, don't tell." I don't know exactly what it pertains to, but it's probably a good idea. In my family, we've had a "Don't ask, don't tell" policy for years, regarding the questionable odor that sometimes occurs around the dinner table after eating refried beans. And while we're on the subject, here's a question that has always bothered me: Why don't Mexicans eat beans the first time they fry them?

WATERBOARDING

And here's another military-related issue. I don't understand this controversy about terrorist prisoners and waterboarding, like at that Geronimo Bay detention center. I don't care whether it's waterboarding, Jet Skis, or body surfing, those prisoners are lucky we let them engage in any sports activities at all! But rest assured, I will keep the military in a state of readiness to confront the asses of evil, wherever they may be.

And here's a little bit of presidential trivia for you about a well-known U.S. military leader and U.S. president. General Ulysses S. Grant, who was known to take a drink every now and then, was the only U.S. president who ever vetoed a bill by throwing up on it.

Credit: William Wade

* * * * * * * * * * *

ATTENTION

**THOSE OF YOU WHO ARE STILL IN THE STORE.
I THINK YOU'VE BEEN HERE LONG ENOUGH.
DOES THE WORD *FREELOADER* MEAN
ANYTHING TO YOU?**

(I knew we should have shrink-wrapped this sucker!)

* * * * * * * * * * *

PROTECTING OUR BORDERS

*Y*ou know, America is supposed to be a "melting pot," but our immigration policy is such a crock, it's more like a Crock-Pot. We ought to run this place like Disneyland. To enter, you would buy a ticket and wait in line for several hours before you can come in and have some fun. The biggest problem is at our border with Mexico. I'll tell you how we solve the problem at our border. It's simple. Build senior citizen housing all along the American side. No one sees more than a nosy old lady peeking through her window blinds.

PHONE SURVEILLANCE

I have no problem with phone surveillance. As any mother can tell you, you can learn a lot of valuable information by listening in on the extension while one of your kids is talking on the phone. That's my kind of intelligence gathering. Although, with the knuckleheads at *my* house, I never really gathered anything you'd call intelligent.

The only people who are giving themselves emotional wedgies over phone surveillance are those bozos at the ACLU. I say you shouldn't care who's listening in on your phone calls unless you have something to hide. I'm not embarrassed about anything I've ever said on the phone, except for a few anonymous calls I made before

Credit: William Wade

they came up with that damn caller ID. Now people can see who's calling, so you have to be careful, no matter how much you want to curse out some bonehead and hang up quick. Of course, these days, with so many people using e-mail, the phone is really only for keeping tabs on your family and sharing gossip you wouldn't want to put in writing. And so what if the government is listening? Do you really think the hallways of the Pentagon will be buzzing over the little tramp you saw going into the Motel 8 with your neighbor's husband? (Three times last week, as best as I could determine from my vantage point.)

As your chief executive, I plan to make sure we continue to do good, old-fashioned phone surveillance. I may even listen in a little myself on a slow day, so keep it clean.

Now if only we could get those illegal aliens to be on the phone while they're crossing the border. Then we'd have it made.

AIRPORT SECURITY

No one likes going through that security system at the airport. Well, I have a plan to make your airport experience less stressful and actually more rewarding. Let's take the security line we all enter on our way to the gate. As you know, we are required to take our shoes off, for security reasons. Sure, it's annoying, and sure, the floor is probably crawling with bacteria, but we must make the best of it. Well, here comes my plan. As long as we have to take our shoes off, I will install a shoe-buffing brush inside the X-ray machine so your shoes will get a little shine as they go through. As you walk through the metal detector, you will feel an invigorating spray of Lysol to cover up your stinky B.O. on the plane. And I haven't forgotten those poor suckers who get pulled out of line for that extra security check and pat down. Attached to the security guy's electronic wand will be a lint brush so you can appear to have some class as you're sandwiched into your coach seat to Cincinnati. Once again, this candidate's watching your back.

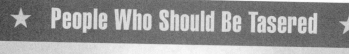

★ **People Who Should Be Tasered** ★

Celebrities who name their children after fruit.

Emergency Preparedness

*A*nd now I must talk about the state of emergency preparedness in this country, starting with that organization known as FEMA, which to me stands for "Federal Expenses Mismanaged Again." The president has said that FEMA is ready to handle emergencies. And if you believe that, you believe Mike Tyson has never smelled pepper spray.

Commonsense Answers from Your Candidate

THE QUESTION: What are some of the things you can eat in an emergency?

MY ANSWER: Leaves, wild berries, and Chicken McNuggets.

I propose that our emergency response systems be taken away from FEMA and turned over to the experts who actually have the resources and determination to respond quickly. I'm talking about Domino's and Pizza Hut. Not only will they show up within a half hour, but they could probably even give starving disaster victims a good deal on those promotional bread sticks.

There are many kinds of emergencies that your federal government must be prepared for, from war and disease to natural disasters like tornadoes, earthquakes, droughts, volcanoes, and hurricanes. For some reason, hurricanes are named after people, yet I have never seen a hurricane named "Thelma." But I don't feel slighted. I once had a sandwich named after me at a coffee shop that ended up being been closed by the board of health. That one sandwich caused more damage to my name than any hurricane could. So I don't care if there's ever a Hurricane Thelma. Besides, I wouldn't particularly enjoy hearing a TV anchor man say, "Thelma's wind breaks . . . film at eleven."

Mama for President

Standing out in a crowd is good, unless you're a lobster.

In addition to counting on the federal government, citizens must take steps to prepare themselves for emergencies. And to do so, everyone should have an emergency supply kit complete with drinking water, food, first aid, and other essentials like Polygrip, Metamucil, and Ben Gay. The main thing is not to panic and start hoarding emergency supplies because someone threw a scare into you. Only a darn fool would get caught up in something like that. So use common sense and just buy what you need. And speaking of emergency supplies; if any of you could use some duct tape, I have about three hundred rolls I'd be happy to let go of pretty cheap.

Once again, just be prepared, and don't worry. If some scary emergency arises while I am president, you can count on me to remain calm as I'm taken to some secret location to change my underwear and assess the situation.

I will have the only platform that looks out for senior citizens. That's right, senior citizens! If I'm elected president, every public restroom will have a grandpa changing station, it will be all right to leave your left turn blinker on for as long as you please, and there will be free back surgery for any old geezer who gets himself wedged inside his Craftmatic Adjustable Bed. Have you seen those damn things on TV? Even Madonna hasn't been in that many positions.

We've all seen those old people riding around on those little scooters. Hey, if that's the only way you can get around, it's okay. But I have an idea. Why not attach a grass-cutting blade on the bottom and put the old fogies to good use? That's right, send Grandpa out for a little ride in the backyard. If Grandpa's not the gardening type, how about a paper route? Gasoline ain't cheap, you know.

I don't see anything wrong with senior citizens continuing to work, as long as it's the right kind of job. But what is the story with that one seventy-year-old employee at every McDonald's? Is that any way to spend your golden years, standing next to Skippy at the french fry machine?

I believe you're never too old for romance, so I will encourage relationships for seniors. Senior citizens actually fall in love the same way as teenagers. The only difference is, seniors take an hour longer to get in and out of the backseat of a car.

Something popular with men right now, and especially seniors, is Viagra. People have asked me, "Mama, what do you think of men taking Viagra?" Well, I don't see anything wrong with putting a snake through some old plumbing. But be careful. Don't be like this one old fool I heard about. Instead of taking Viagra, he took Vigoro, the fertilizer. Not only is he still impotent, but now his hair is growing faster than he can cut it.

There are many great senior citizens in America. One of my favorites is Mr. Larry King. Mr. King is a fine senior citizen, a good interviewer, and quite a ladies' man. Larry is married to a much younger woman, and they have two young sons, even though he's well over seventy. It's good to know that oyster-flavored Metamucil

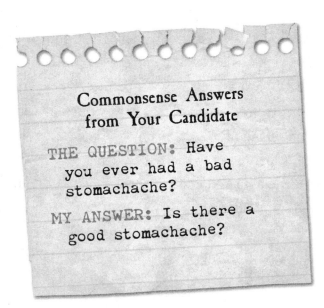

Commonsense Answers
from Your Candidate

THE QUESTION: Have you ever had a bad stomachache?

MY ANSWER: Is there a good stomachache?

really works. Imagine conceiving children at Larry's age. It was probably the first time a man in his seventies actually prayed for stiffness in one of his joints.

I am also fond of another TV host, Mr. Regis Filbert. I have been watching him on TV for many years and would hate to think how old he must be. It's true he is sometimes cranky, but you would be, too, if you had to sit in the makeup chair as long as it probably takes to make Mr. Filbert look presentable at his age.

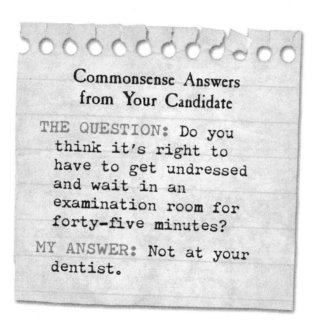

Commonsense Answers from Your Candidate

THE QUESTION: Do you think it's right to have to get undressed and wait in an examination room for forty-five minutes?

MY ANSWER: Not at your dentist.

Another senior citizen who I admire is no longer with us. I'm talking about the popcorn guy Orville Redenbacher. A little-known fact about Orville: In accordance with his wishes, upon his demise he was neither buried nor cremated. They put him in a large microwave.

SAME-SEX MARRIAGE

*M*any people ask me, "Mama, where do you stand on same-sex marriage?" You know, I was married once in my life—Lord rest his soul—and my feeling is, if you want to be as miserable as I was, go ahead and get yourself married. But here's something for you to think about: if you've got one man married to another man, now you've got TWO idiots in the car, both of whom are willing to drive around for three hours before they'll stop to ask for directions!!

STRAIGHTENING OUT OUR YOUNG PEOPLE

When I am president I will use my leadership to straighten out some of our young people. For example, I'm concerned about the way young girls dress, wearing those little skintight lowrider jeans, with a bare midriff and the precious little tattoos. It's disgusting! Half of them even go off to school dressed that way. What the hell are they studying? Lap dancing? And who ever said the belly button is a thing of beauty to be displayed? It is nothing more than a wrinkled little lint collector whose sole purpose in life is to show you where your belt buckle goes—something some of you older gentlemen out there seem to have forgotten. I'll tell you another thing that drives me crazy. Have you seen those young girls with those little skirts that are so darn short? For heaven's sake! If a breeze comes up at all, it's Hello Kitty!

And another thing about the young people out there. Why do they keep getting their bodies pierced? Don't we already have enough openings, holes, and cavities on our bodies? Who needs more? There's a young girl in my neighborhood who got herself pierced a few times. She has so many holes on her body, she's attracting gophers. To the young people, I say forget this nonsense, but if you have made the stupid decision to get a body piercing, at least

Commonsense Answers from Your Candidate

THE QUESTION: What's the best hair-removal device out there?

MY ANSWER: A Band-Aid you've had on for two days or more.

think about where you're getting it done. Remember: when you get pierced at the mall, the employees who do the piercing are probably working there because they weren't smart enough to get hired at McDonald's.

Americans and Their Appearance

*L*ord knows I support a person's desire to look good. But I think we should do something about all these women getting their breasts enlarged. You know, I'm not for that myself. Of course, once you get to be my age, you're not as concerned with size as direction. But I'll tell you what I really don't understand. I don't understand these little skinny gals who get these great big fake things put on that don't even look remotely real. They look like Tinker Bell with bolt-ons. I don't know why they're so popular with you men. You get a little too frisky with those suckers, and you're liable to chip a tooth.

But I wouldn't outlaw all cosmetic surgery. In fact, I will support the idea to put a tax on all cosmetic surgery procedures. It would be called a *vanity tax*. If you think about it, the revenue from Joan Rivers alone could bail out the entire Social Security system.

And let's examine a men's issue for a moment. I don't understand men's designer clothes. You've got Polo, with their logo of a guy on a polo pony. And Nautica, with the picture of a sailboat. Call me crazy, but I don't know too many men who play polo *or* have a sailboat. I think someone should come out with a line of designer clothes for the average man. Their logo on the pocket would be a guy sitting on the toilet, reading the Sunday paper.

And then there are men's accessories. Something I don't understand is why an overweight, middle-aged traveling salesman would possibly need a Navy Seals watch. Maybe the pool at the Ramada Inn is deeper than I thought.

★ VOTE FOR ★

Questions the Other Candidates Aren't Asking:

When you buy hair spray, which is stronger—Maximum Hold, Ultra Hold, Mega Hold, or Super Hold?

★ ★ MAMA ★ ★

There are many issues that have been neglected by all of the other candidates throughout the history of our country. I, Thelma Harper, plan to tackle some of those issues. For example, if elected president, I will outlaw those automatic toilets that flush three times before you can get your pants back up! It happened to me again the other day at the airport. I swear I got splashed more times than a head of lettuce at Wal-Mart.

I want my citizens to become better consumers. You must stay alert and vigilant when you're out there shopping, and ask yourself the hard questions. For example, why do car dealers have a sign showing us the "Salesman of the Month"? Isn't that the guy to stay away from?

And here's a question for all of my fellow Americans. Why the hell do stores make you show your ID on every credit card purchase, even if it's only five dollars? If I stole a credit card, would my big score be Rolaids and some batteries? I don't think so.

And speaking of products, there are some consumer products I don't understand at all, like "Jockey Shorts for *Her*." Unless women have changed in some way I don't know about, aren't those going to be kind of roomy in the front?

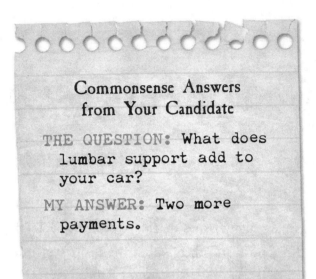

Commonsense Answers
from Your Candidate

THE QUESTION: What does
lumbar support add to
your car?

MY ANSWER: Two more
payments.

Here's a question for you: Why does a backscratcher have to have that stupid little *hand* on the end? Are they afraid we would think it's a long fork and set the table with it?

And in the supermarket, have you seen those machines that they rent for steam cleaning your carpets? Lord, I hate those things. You ever rent one of those? You turn it on and watch the water spinning around behind the glass. It's nothing more than a blender on wheels. It doesn't clean worth a damn, but it leaves tracks everywhere, so it makes you feel like you did something. Next time, just drag a chair back and forth across the carpet and save yourself some money.

Here's a good one. I read that Costco recently started selling caskets. Now, I love Costco, but you know how it is in there. You're not going to be able to put Grandpa into the box unless he's got that darn membership card in his pocket. Leave it to Costco. Next they'll

Going to that great membership club in the sky

be selling that twelve-pack of Duraflame logs as the do-it-yourself cremation kit!

And what the hell's wrong with the advertising people? Like, whoever came up with that McDonald's character the "Hamburglar"? Is a burglar really a good role model for children? What's next? The French Fry Forger? The Flame-Broiled Arsonist? Before you know it, they'll have our kids singing along with Big and Tasty, the Flasher! Now, that's one set of McNuggets I don't want to see!

Speaking of advertising, have you seen the commercial for Combat Roach Killing Gel? Why the devil is it a gel? I want to waste the little suckers, not style their hair!

I may become the first president who can actually offer advice to homemakers. Care for a homemaking tip? Besides being a well-known snack food, Cheez Whiz also makes an excellent caulk.

Commonsense Answers
from Your Candidate

THE QUESTION: Mama, my husband's birthday is coming, and I have forty dollars put aside to buy him a watch. But I don't want to sound dumb in the store. So please tell me . . . that watch company spelled S-e-i-k-o: Is it pronounced "SEE-ko" or "SAY-ko"?

MY ANSWER: Very simple, sweetie . . . for forty dollars, it's pronounced "Timex."

Business in America

$\mathcal{F}$ ree enterprise is the American way. Many companies show dedication and persistence in pursuing their goals and carving out their spot in the marketplace, in spite of challenging odds. One case in point is the Publisher's Clearing House. You've all seen their representatives charging up to someone's front door with an oversized check. In spite of the millions of dollars in prize money given away by the Publisher's Clearing House, not one person has ever ordered a magazine from them, but it hasn't stopped them.

And here's another company with a lot of determination: Kinko's. They have huge stores, lots of big, expensive machines, and dozens of employees, and the average customer only spends forty cents, but they persist. Good for you, Kinko's!

Have you seen those pharmacies with drive-thru windows? It's not a bad idea, but they're running them too much like the drive-thru restaurants. The other day, I drove through for a prescription, and the voice said, "Do you want some suppositories with that?"

I heard that the PetSmart company had opened a pet hotel. Now, is this really necessary? Dogs spend each day eating, sleeping, and sniffing themselves. It's not like they need to go on vacation. And I don't know of a single dog or cat that travels for business. What the hell are they going to do at a pet hotel that they can't do at home? And how would you like to work in a place like that? I don't know about you, but I always leave a couple of dollars on the table for the chambermaid. I'd hate to find out what a dog would leave.

I believe we need to return to a simpler time. For example, let's look at that health club known as "24 Hour Fitness." Did you know they're open all night? Who the devil needs to do deep knee bends and squats at three in the morning? The only time you need to squat at three in the morning is if you're camping and you're too far from the outdoor john.

There are many questionable business practices that I will be looking into. For one, I will make it illegal for a Beverly Hills plastic surgeon to repossess breasts that haven't been paid for.

And let's talk about a shady business practice that I'm going to do something about. You know those advertisements you receive in the

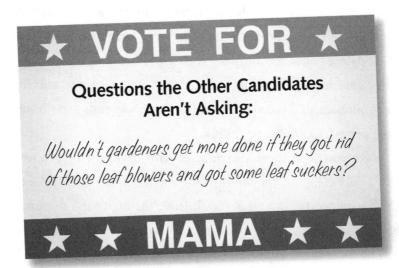

★ VOTE FOR ★

Questions the Other Candidates Aren't Asking:

Wouldn't gardeners get more done if they got rid of those leaf blowers and got some leaf suckers?

★ ★ MAMA ★ ★

mail, with bogus checks that look real but say, "This is not a check"? I'm going to fix it so you can cash those checks! That little scam will disappear faster than a sumo wrestler's thong.

Commonsense Answers from Your Candidate

THE QUESTION: If you're in a public bathroom and someone helps you, how much should you tip them?

MY ANSWER: First, I'd make sure the person actually works there.

A Balanced Budget

*I*t is important for America to have a balanced budget. And there are many steps we can take to manage the country's finances. For starters, I will close the federal government's bank account wherever it is now and open a new one at a bank that gives a free gift with a new account. A free toaster or tote bag would be nice. Furthermore, I will be sure our national checking account does not have any overdraft protection because that stupid stuff makes it too easy to spend past your means. When we need some funds to bail out an airline or mortgage company, the treasury secretary will wait in line at the ATM machine, just like all of you less important citizens. And I promise he or she will not attempt to cut in line or look over your shoulder while you are getting some cash for the weekend.

Furthermore, I will open us a credit card with an airline miles rebate for all those foreign trips the secretary of state makes to hobnob with foreigners. And you can rest assured that we will make

America
Washington, DC

Date _____

Pay to the
Order of _____ $ _____

_____ Dollars

For *Something Important*   *President Thelma Harper*

⑆00000000000⑆ 00000000000000⑈ 0 000

Credit: William Wade and BigStockPhoto

sure to use those free miles so we don't end up redeeming them for fishing magazines (or other junk) when they're about to expire.

If all of the measures I take fail to balance our budget, I'll do what any other sensible senior in my position would do: take out a reverse mortgage on the White House. See how far a little common sense will take you? No thank-yous are necessary.

Mama for President

Never compromise your principles for money . . . without getting some up front.

Commonsense Answers
from Your Candidate

THE QUESTION: I want to go into politics. I'm hardworking, honest, and principled. I don't believe in stepping on others and want to succeed on my own merits. Any advice?

MY ANSWER: Yes. Give it up. You don't stand a chance.

For many of you, taxes are a big issue. But taxes are a necessary evil. If you get a good tax preparer, you can avoid paying a lot of taxes, and maybe avoid paying taxes completely. (Don't tell anyone you heard that from me.) Yes, people will try all different ways to avoid paying taxes. But I will crack down on this.

No one likes to receive an audit notice. So I will do something to ease the pain. In order to make it more pleasant, we will do it like the Publisher's Clearing House, the people I was talking about before. If you owe money, we will knock on your door with balloons, a TV crew, and an oversized check. The amount filled in will be what you owe. All you'll have to do is sign the check with an oversized magic marker. Bingo! We get our money, and you avoid going to jail and becoming a love slave to a large man named Ratzo. And as a gesture of goodwill, you will be allowed to keep the balloons. As for paying off the amount you owe, instead of just giving you one huge lump sum to fret over, we will have compassion and handle it like those TV infomercials, allowing you to turn over your life savings in "three easy payments."

And now let me share some advice for all of you taxpayers out there. Number one: avoid a tax preparer whose brochure refers to him as a "model prisoner." Two, no matter how unfair you think your tax situation is, always keep your anger in check. When answering a letter from the IRS, never begin your response with the words "Dear Bloodsuckers."

As your president, I will tell the IRS to investigate tax fraud to the fullest extent of the law. For example, tax-exempt status is given to legitimate churches. You are not a church just because you have a velvet picture of the Last Supper over your sofa.

You can, however, legitimately reduce your tax bill by making charitable contributions; you will also enjoy the satisfaction you will receive from giving to charity. As your president, I will encourage people to give to worthwhile organizations not only to save on taxes but also to assist the less fortunate and disadvantaged. I believe for example, that we must help the homeless, or as I refer to them, the "hygiene-challenged." But I urge all citizens to carefully investigate all charitable organizations. For example, I keep hearing commercials about donating your car to the blind. I'm not sure that's such a good idea. I'd prefer they keep walking with those dogs.

Another way to reduce your taxes is to claim dependents, who are usually members of your family. Most dependents are young children. Some young adults are still dependents. If, however, your son is over the age of thirty and is still listed on your tax return, the technical term for him is "Loser."

I probably shouldn't be giving you any tax saving ideas. The U.S. Treasury needs your tax money in order to operate the government. Imagine how much it costs to keep Washington running. Take the Congressional dining room. Ted Kennedy's lunch bill alone is probably in the millions.

As candidates have done in the past, I plan to make my tax returns public for all to see. (Note to the IRS: regarding the dress I donated to Goodwill last year that I valued at $350, please make that $6. Oops!)

Speaking of taxes, you know the expression "There's nothing more certain than death and taxes." Well, I found one more, y'all. When the phone rings again, right after a wrong number, you can be certain it's the same damn moron!

Commonsense Answers from Your Candidate

THE QUESTION: When is it unnecessary to file an accident report with the police?

MY ANSWER: When the accident in question took place nine months ago in your bedroom.

*I*n my opinion, it's about time the White House got a makeover. For one thing, I don't like the exterior paint color. White is so impractical. Perhaps a nice pastel would be pleasant. And I'm thinking some of those rolling shutters would be good—they're supposed to keep burglars away, you know. But the problem is that we can't spend too much money. Well, don't worry, because I have the perfect solution: instead of reaching into the taxpayers' pockets, I will get us and another country booked on an episode of that TV show *Trading Spaces*. The only problem will be finding the right country. For example, Spain is a nice country. No, on second thought, not Spain. I'm not coming home to find a velvet bullfighter on the wall in the Lincoln Bedroom.

How about Sweden? No, forget Sweden. We're liable to end up with some of that cheap-looking junk from IKEA. I don't even think that stuff's made of real wood.

I've got it. We'll go on *Trading Spaces* with Russia. What a great step toward reinforcing our superiority over the Ruskies, for the world to see Dmitry Medvedev on a ladder, painting my crown molding. If for any reason we can't get on that show, I'll just do what any other sensible person would do: wait for the first big sale at Levitz and put some practical items in the White House, like some nice simulated-leather recliners, a card table and chairs, and possibly a sleeper sofa in the Oval Office for the vice president. But no "nesting tables." Have you seen those things? Who's the moron who came up with "nesting tables"? You know, those little end tables stacked one on top of the other. Why the hell do I need two more tables underneath my table? You can only put something on the top one! And they make you buy all three. Who's that little short one for? Your dog? My dog doesn't play cards, he doesn't do jigsaw puzzles, and he doesn't sit at the table for his meals. He eats out of our garbage cans and drinks out of the toilet, for heaven's sake. Just sell me an end table and stop screwing with me!

Credit: Photos.com

"Nesting Tables"—give me a break!

As far as the Oval Office is concerned, I won't make a lot of changes. For one thing, I will keep the large wooden desk that several other presidents have used. I'm not sure what kind of wood it's made of. But I like all kinds of wood, especially oak, pine, and monogamy. In addition to some paintings, there are currently three busts in the Oval Office. I guess once I'm elected, there will be four. (I hope you don't mind me making a little joke.)

I will continue to allow White House tours, but I will make some changes to them. For one thing, I will start serving refreshments. I don't think you should have someone over and not offer them anything. So I will put out some chips, Diet Rite Cola, and a small dish of Jell-O, probably cherry. I sometimes like making an onion dip with sour cream and Lipton's onion soup, which I will do for the tour visitors, if I have time.

Credit: Heavenly Perspective Photography

Mix 1 envelope Lipton onion soup mix and 1 container of sour cream, and watch for the smiles (and crumbs).

There will be a small charge for the White House tour in order to clean the carpet occasionally and repair the linoleum in the kitchen, if it's scratched. But I'll tell you now: don't expect to see a lot of fancy stuff on display. I don't want to be responsible for any expensive antiques, so we'll sock those away at Public Storage, and I'll bring some of my own things over, although probably not my bobblehead collection. Sorry.

Once I take over, to make people feel more at home, we will have a greeter at the front door of the White House, just like they have at Wal-Mart. And on the way out, visitors will have to walk through one of those electronic railings that will ring if some visiting ambassador tries to steal some towels or an ashtray.

* * * * * * * * * * *

ATTENTION

STRAGGLERS AND HARD-CORE BROWSERS!
PLEASE DON'T LET ME FIND OUT YOU'RE STILL
IN THE STORE, READING THIS THING. THE BEST
THINGS IN LIFE MAY BE FREE, BUT NOT MY BOOK.
GET A MOVE ON. SECURITY!

* * * * * * * * * * *

*A*lthough I haven't decided on my entire cabinet yet, I have made some important selections already. For example, my choice for attorney general will be Miss Nancy Grace, God bless her. She won't take any crap from anybody. And not only will she be a fine attorney general, dispatching the bad guys to their just rewards, but she'll be easier to protect because, for starters, I believe her hair is bulletproof. I'll even let her keep her TV show as long as she keeps saving us money by trying all those important cases on CNN.

Another important position to fill is secretary of state. That person is in charge of keeping tabs on other countries and making sure they do what we tell them. It takes someone who likes to travel to exotic lands and doesn't mind foreigners too much. And I have come up with a person who has all of these qualities and some sex appeal to boot. (There's nothing wrong with a little eye candy to spruce up our image in the world.) So for secretary of state, I'm nominating that globe-trotting *Tomb Raider*, Miss Angelina Jolie. With a gal like her in charge, we'll have foreign leaders lining up to sign treaties. It'll be a new era in American diplomacy. And I'm so confident she's the woman for the job, I already have plans to buy ten or twenty bunk beds for the White House in case she wants to bring all her children for a sleepover.

And then there's the treasury secretary. This person must be able to manage the affairs of our massive U.S. treasury and put their signature on all new dollar bills, which is probably very time consuming. As secretary of the treasury, I would nominate a smart gal who is probably careful with money. I'm talking about Miss Whoopi Goldberg. I don't know her personal finances, but from what I've seen, she certainly doesn't waste a lot of money on clothes.

★ **People Who Should Be Tasered** ★

People at the supermarket who start eating their groceries before they pay for them. It's a supermarket, not a restaurant!

And as you know, I believe education is important, so I want someone hard-working, smart, and dedicated as secretary of education. Who better for education than a woman who rose from humble beginnings to have her own book club? Of course I'm talking about Miss Oprah Winfrey. This appointment will not only be good for the country, it will also be good for Oprah because an impressive position like this might be just the thing to get a marriage proposal out of that longtime boyfriend of hers, and wouldn't that be nice! Running the education department with its annual budget of 59 billion dollars will be a great opportunity for Oprah, unless she feels it's a step down to be in control of less money than she's used to.

My choice for secretary of defense may surprise you. My fellow Americans, for secretary of defense, we need someone tough, so I would nominate Miss Martha Stewart. Don't be fooled by the charm she projects from behind that apron. She's General Patton with a spatula. She tries to come across warm and friendly . . . sure. Until you burn the soufflé. Then she'll roast your ass like a Cornish hen on Christmas. I remember hearing that she came out of jail kinder and gentler. All I can say is, how rough was that gal to begin with if a stretch in the slammer actually brought out her softer side?

Because of the bad experiences every homeowner and landlord has ever had, I have also decided on a *new* cabinet-level position: *Painting Contractor of the United States.* He will supervise all estimates and make sure your painter shows up. He will also be the only cabinet-level official who will not be paid until his job is done.

I will evaluate all of the remaining cabinet positions and maybe even eliminate some of them. For example, there's the secretary of the interior, currently a Mr. Dirk Kempthorne, who I'm not so sure about. I have not seen Dirk's interior designs even once on Home and Garden Television. So exactly what are Mr. Kempthorne's qualifications, and how much does he know about interiors? Can he turn "trash to treasure"? Can he "design on a dime"? To get to the bottom of this, I intend to thoroughly probe Mr. Kempthorne, although not physically of course. After a complete investigation, we may find that we can eliminate this cabinet position and some of the others, and get a smaller conference table.

Health Care

The nation's health and well-being are especially important to me. And so, as your president, I will devote resources to combating dangerous diseases. For example, I am quite concerned about the West Nile virus, which is spread by mosquitoes. I hate those little bastards. They sneak up on you and suck your blood. They're like lawyers with wings. As your president, I intend to launch an all-out U.S. military attack on the little buggers, and they'll never bite my American butt again!

Prevention is important when it comes to health care, so I will encourage all Americans to get flu shots. Flu shots are nothing to be afraid of. Recently a woman I met said, "Mama, my husband is smart and good-looking, but he's a real chicken about getting a flu shot. Where is a better place for the shot: on the arm or on a butt cheek?" I told her that depends on whether you're getting one or just watching.

We have learned many things that will contribute to better health overall. For example, we have learned that children who are breast-fed have fewer cavities. However, if your kids are already in high school, just get them a toothbrush and some dental floss.

Commonsense Answers
from Your Candidate

THE QUESTION: Is
chicken soup really
good for your health?

MY ANSWER: Yes, unless
you're a chicken.

Many Americans are overweight and turning to the weight-loss industry for answers. For example, last year, more than 25,000 people had their stomachs stapled. Of those, 24,999 did it to lose weight. The one remaining guy did it after getting drunk in his company's office-supply room.

Yes, obesity is a problem in America. There was even a law proposed in one state that would've ordered restaurants to stop serving obese people. Is this the right approach? I don't think so. Were this law to have been passed, I can only imagine a gang of fat people marching for their civil rights, chanting "We shall overeat." And we don't need that. So I don't believe it is right to ban obese people from restaurants. Buffets, however, are a different story. We all know there are too many obese people at buffets. They congregate there like elephants at the watering hole. At least elephants leave something for the vultures. So when it comes to the buffet, I say boot out the obese customers, and maybe there will be some shrimp left over for the rest of us. If that is too extreme, let's allow them in from 5 PM to 6 PM and call it "Fatty Hour." Problem solved.

★ VOTE FOR ★

Questions the Other Candidates Aren't Asking:

Do you have to have cold hands to be a nurse?

★ ★ MAMA ★ ★

Speaking of being overweight, here's something I don't understand: *The Subway Diet.* How in the heck are you supposed to lose weight eating a foot-long loaf of bread three times a day?

By the way, before I forget about those buffets, I've got another idea. I'm going to see that they remove those stupid glass sneeze-guards that are supposed to protect the food. Heck, old people usually put their fingers in the bowls anyway. So all that glass is doing is getting in our way and giving the rest of you a false sense of security.

But back to health care, let's talk about our hospitals. This is an area of health care that needs reforming, especially when it comes to the costs. When was the last time you stayed in a hospital? It's something like $2,000 a night, and sometimes they don't even have cable.

And we all know the cost of prescription drugs is out of control. I

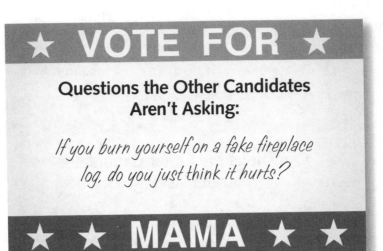

★ **VOTE FOR** ★

Questions the Other Candidates Aren't Asking:

If you burn yourself on a fake fireplace log, do you just think it hurts?

★ ★ **MAMA** ★ ★

was just talking about this with my pharmacist last week while I was putting some Prevacid on layaway.

I even have a proposal that would benefit young people in line at the pharmacy counter behind a senior citizen. I'm going to suggest

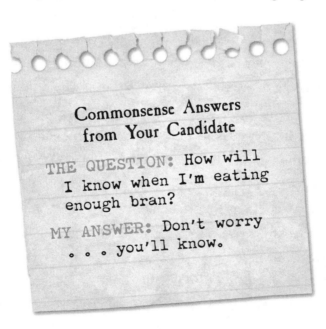

Commonsense Answers
from Your Candidate

THE QUESTION: How will
I know when I'm eating
enough bran?

MY ANSWER: Don't worry
. . . you'll know.

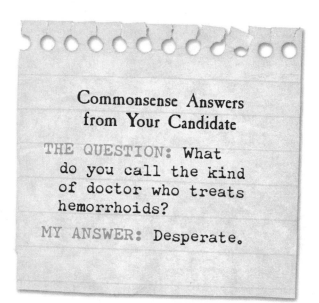

Commonsense Answers
from Your Candidate

THE QUESTION: What
do you call the kind
of doctor who treats
hemorrhoids?

MY ANSWER: Desperate.

for every pharmacy where old people go, they put in an express window for eight prescriptions or less.

People say our whole health care system is broken. Well, let me tell you right now that the problem with our health care system is that the laws are all made by healthy people. If we had more people in Congress coughing, wheezing, and limping around, they might have the motivation to get some decent health care laws passed. And that's where *I* come in. I've got enough aches and pains to push through comprehensive health care for every man, woman, and child in America.

The Environment

GLOBAL WARMING

I've been asked what I would do about global warming. This is a subject I know a lot about. As a postmenopausal woman, my globes have experienced a lot of warming. So, for discussion purposes, let's think of global warming as kind of a transatlantic hot flash.

This global warming will supposedly raise the temperatures at the North and South Poles and melt the ice. Big deal. We can always buy more ice. Seven-Eleven sells a bag of cubes for $1.99. I think everyone's making too big a deal about this global-warming thing. It's probably just temporary. So it warms up a bit. Get out your culottes and bermuda shorts. And crank up the SPF. Who's afraid of a little heat? I have always found the breeze from a window fan on a hot day to be the best way to cool off on the porch in a comfortable rocking chair.

This is the greatest country on earth, with the greatest technological minds. I will put those minds to work on a plan I have to place giant window fans on some of our tallest buildings to combat global warming and create a delightful breeze for future generations to enjoy.

All it takes is a little good, old-fashioned know-how.

So to all of those global-warming crybabies, let's look on the bright side. Sure, the oceans may be heating up, but there's a benefit for us gals in the kitchen. Just think of all the time you'll save boiling water. And if the oceans are heating up as they say, we'll someday be able to catch fish that are already steamed and ready to eat. Think of all the possibilities.

Besides, global warming can't be as bad as they say, or how could the winters be so severe? Last December where I live, it was so cold, my cable guy had frost on his butt crack. So much for your global warming!

AIR POLLUTION

Air pollution and its effect on us is ~~insideous incideous~~ very bad. As your candidate, I know something has to be done about our air quality. This morning I saw a dog chasing a cat, and they were both walking.

Some places have worse air than others. Especially hard-hit is Los Angeles, the only place I know where cigarette smoke actually *improves* the air quality.

This is a difficult problem to deal with because bad air is colorless and odorless. It's the vodka of pollution. (By the way, I don't drink hard liquor, although I do have a beer occasionally—strictly for medicinal purposes.)

In order to improve our air, one candidate has been talking about something called "green-collar" jobs. That must be something new. Usually, the only time you have a green collar is when you're using the cheap generic detergent.

It's a fact that much of our air pollution is caused by automobiles. So some experts have said we should leave our cars at home and find alternative modes of transportation, like riding a bicycle.

Unfortunately, that one's not for me. The last time a woman my age was seen riding a bicycle was in *The Wizard of Oz*. And you all know what happened to *her*.

Air pollution is not only outside; it's also a serious indoor problem. To combat indoor air pollution, you can try buying that silent air purifier from that store with all the fancy gadgets. I'm talking about that tall skinny machine that looks like an anorexic room fan. This device supposedly draws something called negative eons onto a shiny metal stick, but probably the most impressive thing it does is draw thousands of dollars into the cash register at that gadget store. I have a different concept for keeping the air clean at home. It's called *dusting*.

I'm not saying I am against technological advances to fight air pollution. In fact, I have already bought one of those light bulbs that's all twisted like a pretzel. Have you seen those? They look like the guy at GE got drunk at the light bulb machine.

Planting trees is also good for our air. The reason for this is too complicated for you to understand. Let's just say that trees suck up the bad air and spit good air out at us, not to mention that trees class up the neighborhood and provide shelter for birds and other wildlife. Just be careful standing under a tree with a bird in it. The air may be clean, but the top of your head won't be.

CONSERVATION

Many people talk about conservation of the rain forests. Rain forests are the places where you find tribes of people in loincloths, weaving baskets and spearing fish for dinner. They lack many of the things we take for granted, like plumbing, electricity, and *teeth*. From the looks of their loincloths and mud shacks, they may have gone a little overboard on the conservation. If I was one of those people in the rain forest, instead of baskets, I might want to think about weaving myself an *umbrella*. But I think I have a solution for the people of the rain forest. I think it's time to bring them a Wal-Mart and a McDonald's. And maybe a dentist wouldn't be a bad idea. If there isn't a dentist available to set up shop, let the Wal-Mart eyeglasses guy do it. It's not like they're going to know the difference.

And here's some advice for you that may come in handy: if you believe Styrofoam is not environmentally friendly, rice cakes make great packing material.

Mama for President

If a tree falls in the forest and there is no one there to hear it, wouldn't it still tick off all those environmentalists?

These days you hear a lot of talk about our energy policies—especially the price of gas. I, too, will add my voice to the debate. And I am no Thelma-come-lately to this subject. Remember, I'm an old woman, and I've been getting gas for a long time. Take it from me—you shouldn't be surprised by what you're paying at the gas station. What do you expect from a place that even charges for *air*?

But the price of gasoline is ridiculous. Last week, at the gas station, I asked the attendant for a dollar's worth, and he let me sniff the pump. These gas prices just aren't right. For what they're doing to us, we should get dinner and a movie first.

And aren't they the clever ones? The other day, I was going to complain about the service, and I remembered that I filled up my tank myself. I asked to use the bathroom, and the clerk pointed to a key attached to an anvil. So I just bought a $6 muffin and left.

To save energy, we must get the gas guzzlers off the road. Why the hell does anyone need a Hummer? Who are you—Oliver North? I have been driving a Chevy Nova for many years now, and I can tell you there's plenty of room in there for up to four people, plus two or three bags of groceries and a case of Depends.

Carpooling would be a good idea if it didn't mean being crammed in a car with the same deadbeats you work with all day, so that's pretty much out of the question. What we need to do is come up with alternative fuels. I've had some experience with ethanol, but more as a beverage. I intend to look into it as an alternative fuel. Apparently, alternative fuels can be derived from things like corn and sugarcane. And there's even another one they're working on in Texas. It is a fuel derived from cow manure. (And you think gas station restrooms smell bad *now*.)

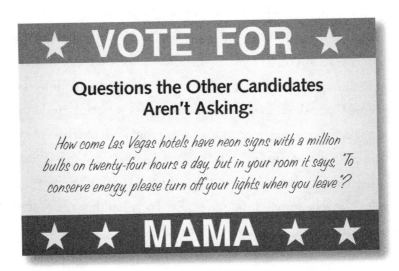

★ VOTE FOR ★

Questions the Other Candidates Aren't Asking:

How come Las Vegas hotels have neon signs with a million bulbs on twenty-four hours a day, but in your room it says, "To conserve energy, please turn off your lights when you leave"?

★ ★ MAMA ★ ★

CLONING

*P*eople have asked me what I think of cloning, which is making an exact copy of yourself without having to rest your butt on the Xerox machine. For any of you who are in favor of human cloning, I have two words for you: *Richard Simmons*! That reminds me: I heard that at one point, Simmons wanted to become a doctor. I don't know. If you ask me, this is not the kind of guy you'd want to see while you're wearing a gown with no back on it. By the way, it's not surprising Richard has never been in a relationship with a woman. The only ones he knows are fat and crying all the time. Dennis Rodman's another strange one. You know, he was the only NBA player with a tampon endorsement. But I digress.

Back on the subject of cloning, I read recently that they have now cloned a horse, which might explain McDonald's Dollar Menu. However, the well-known original cloning experiment was with a sheep, which is attributed to a Scottish scientist. But if you ask me, they're giving credit to the wrong individual. The first person to actually perfect cloning was the mother of those Baldwin brothers.

SPACE PROGRAM

I will support our space program because the exploration of space is a wonderful thing. And space belongs to all of us. As some of you may have heard, average citizens like you and me can actually pay to have a star in the sky named after a loved one. I paid to have a star named after my late husband. But they sent my money back. They said you can't have a star named "Dumb Ass."

As a senior citizen, I was especially proud when former astronaut and senator John Glenn went back into space at the age of seventy-seven. The tensest moment in space for Senator Glenn was when

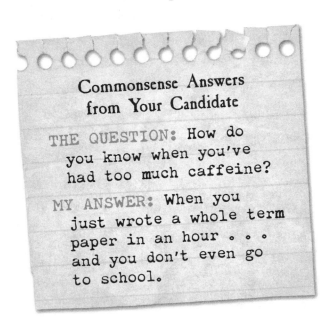

Commonsense Answers
from Your Candidate

THE QUESTION: How do you know when you've had too much caffeine?

MY ANSWER: When you just wrote a whole term paper in an hour . . . and you don't even go to school.

they explained to him that he wasn't on Disney World's parachute ride with his grandchildren. Boy, did he have the shock of his life.

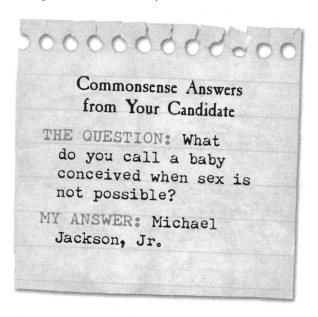

Commonsense Answers from Your Candidate

THE QUESTION: What do you call a baby conceived when sex is not possible?

MY ANSWER: Michael Jackson, Jr.

There are tremendous advances in science being achieved every day, giving new knowledge to us all. Did you know, for example, that when viewed under a microscope, a fat cell looks a lot like Kirstie Alley?

Anyway, once I'm president, I will have scientists working on some of the questions that have gone unanswered for years. For example, if we have a biological clock inside of us, shouldn't one of our hands be longer than the other?

I will have scientists devoting their time to things important to Americans, like developing a way to cool one of those McDonald's apple pies. And here's a bit of trivia for you. The snail can have hundreds of teeth. The same is true of anyone born into the Osmond family.

Commonsense Answers from Your Candidate

THE QUESTION: Mama, I'm a high school student studying for a science exam. What's the smallest object on earth?

MY ANSWER: A parking space marked "compact."

Crime and Punishment

*M*any people are concerned with crime in the streets. Actually our streets are safe. It's on the sidewalk where you can get your butt kicked.

Something that bothers me is our media and the way they report on crime. Some of the reporting is just downright stupid. I saw an article in the newspaper the other day. It said, "A man was found in an alley last night, beaten, stabbed, shot, and poisoned. Police suspect foul play."

Then there's the phrase "career criminal." Crime is not a career. It's what some people do instead of a career.

The job of fighting crime is in the hands of our fine police officers. I, for one, am always glad to see a police officer, unless it's in my rearview mirror. But some of their crime-fighting tools puzzle me. For example, I'm not sure about the effectiveness of our police using pepper spray as a weapon. Do they really think you can stop criminals with *seasoning*? What's next—zucchini nightsticks? Citizens have tried all kinds of ways to protect themselves. Some people even use a recording of dogs barking to scare away intruders. Actually, there's something even better. It's a CD called *William Shatner Sings*.

Speaking of William Shatner singing, crime comes in many forms. I will devote some of my time to defeating what is called white-collar crime, although I think we should give credit to people who at least try to look their best while breaking the law. But while we're on the subject of white-collar crime, I never understood all the fuss about something called "Whitewater." Our real concern should be *yellow* water . . . especially if it's in the swimming pool and it's warmer than the water around it. Regardless, you may rest assured that in my administration, I will reduce political scandals down to a precious few.

Now let's talk about our prisons. Many stupid things happen within our prison system. A while back, I read about a one-legged death-row inmate in Texas who asked for an artificial leg so he could walk to his execution. Isn't that a lot like getting new tires for the demolition derby?

As you know, our prisons are overcrowded, so we need to reduce the number of repeat offenders. To relieve that overcrowding, we should do what I've always done when I've had too many overnight guests. Start vacuuming at about six thirty in the morning. Turn that Hoover up full blast. I think this will reduce the number of repeat offenders in our prison system because, after a whole day of weight lifting and making homemade knives, nothing is worse than being unable to sleep in.

Credit: William Wade and photos.com

★ People Who Should Be Tasered ★

Women who fall in love with convicted murderers in prison. How bad can the dating pool in your neighborhood be for you to have to come on to Hannibal Lechter?

The best deterrent to crime is punishment that truly fits the crime. I offer the following examples:

CRIME	PUNISHMENT
Taking up two parking spaces	Your car gets sawed in half
Taking condiments from fast food restaurants or buying one soda and sharing with others in your party	Owner of restaurant comes to your house and takes whatever he wants out of your cupboards
Using work supplies for personal business	Boss gets to come to your house and clean you out of toilet paper
Bringing an extra person to a wedding or dinner that you didn't RSVP for	Three of the host's relatives move in with you
Identity theft	Identity theft victim takes your identity and signs you up for every book club, polling company, and pyramid scheme in America
Popping wheelies on a street where children are playing	The parents get to remove all four wheels of your car and six of your teeth
Disturbing the peace with your loud party music	Neighbors get to retaliate by amping up Lawrence Welk reruns the following five nights
Allowing your grocery cart to roll into parked cars, instead of returning it to a proper grocery cart cage	Have to volunteer your car for grade school field trips for an entire school year
Grocery checker packs your bread at the bottom of two fireplace starter logs and a gallon of milk	Customer gets to drive over grocery checker's lunch with her SUV

Guns

*P*eople have asked me for my position on firearms, which is covered by the Second Amendment. That's the amendment that gives us the right to keep and bear arms, and blow a deer away with an assault rifle. Well, let me just say, sometimes I wish there were no guns or knives. Then, the worst thing a crook could shove in the face of a convenience store clerk would be one of those Slim Jims or pepperoni sticks. As you know, those items are relatively harmless, unless, of course, you eat one.

There would be many benefits to eliminating the guns out there. For instance, if our hospital emergency rooms weren't so busy with shooting victims and gun accidents, they might have more time for the rest of us. Take it from me; there is nothing worse than having your bunions put on the back burner while a doctor treats some flea-brain who shot off his big toe.

I don't carry a gun, but if elected president, I assume my Secret Service agents will be packing heat. Good Lord, I hope so! I want them armed to the hilt. This is one old gal who's not taking any chances—not with all the crazies who'll be coming out of the woodwork. And I'm just talking about my family. Imagine how many other weirdos are milling around out there.

Commonsense Answers
from Your Candidate

THE QUESTION: I know this is a weird thing to ask, but if you were a condemned prisoner, what would you request for your last meal?

MY ANSWER: Something to go.

Until I am given official protection, be warned that I have Mace in my purse. Try anything funny with me on the campaign trail and you'll be crying harder than Paula Dean during a butter shortage.

Speaking of the campaign trail, I probably won't be doing much close-up handshaking anyway, and not just for my own security. Nothing personal, but there isn't enough hand sanitizer in the world to fight off all of those germs. And don't expect me to kiss any babies. My stomach isn't that strong any more, and some of you folks have given birth to some mighty scary-looking little creatures. Bring them around after they stop drooling and burping. And the same goes for their grandparents. Where was I? Oh yes, guns.

Some people use firearms needlessly, like firing a gun into the air to celebrate the New Year. What are those lug nuts thinking? Unless you managed to hit a pigeon, that bullet's falling back to earth faster than skydiving weightwatchers.

Unfortunately, guns are a part of our culture, and there may not be much we can do about it. Think about our entertainment over the years. How many people would rent a movie called *The Slingshots of Navarone* or *Food-fight at the OK Corral.*

But I'll tell you right now; angry people should not be allowed to have guns. If you're a person with an anger problem, instead of reaching for a gun, you should do what I do when I am annoyed: throw something at the TV (which, by the way, I have been known to do often during Dr. Phil's advice segments). Try my method, and you'll feel better in no time. Whenever I relieve myself in this way, I am filled with the calmness and serenity of that great philosopher, and my fellow author, Mr. Deepak Okra.

Some people use guns for the sport of hunting. I'm not in favor of this. In most other sports, like football, baseball, or tennis, your opponent has a chance against you. So I say, until a deer, a moose, or a duck learns how to operate a high-powered rifle, we should at least stop calling hunting a sport.

But first and foremost, listen to your mama and stop buying toy guns for children. A small, underdeveloped brain has no business near firearms. Just ask that poor fellow who went hunting with Dick Cheney.

By the way, I don't know about that Dick Cheney. He looks like the kind of guy who'd go to Lou Gehrig's farewell speech and heckle.

*H*oliday traditions are important to me. My favorite thing at Christmas is to look at a beautiful Nativity scene, with the wise men bringing gifts. You know, that was the world's first baby shower. And we still have those today. Of course, the gifts have kind of deteriorated from frankincense and myrrh to diapers and a squeeze toy.

I've never understood Presidents' Day, when we honor two of our greatest presidents, George Washington and Abraham Lincoln, by having a sale at the department store. What about a day for some of our other presidents? We could celebrate Ronald Reagan by taking a nap and Richard Nixon by taking a powder.

At the White House, there is a tradition of an Easter egg hunt on the White House lawn. If you ask me, the Easter Bunny has no more place at the White House than other myths, like weapons of mass destruction in Iraq. When I am president, I will end the annual Easter egg hunt because the president shouldn't be hiding things.

That is the job of the vice president's chief of staff. It is much easier to send that person to prison, like in the case of Scooter Libby.

Every year, at Thanksgiving, the president pardons a turkey. I have no problem with that. It's the turkeys that presidents have appointed to run federal agencies, like FEMA, that bother me.

By the way, here's a little bit of holiday trivia for you. It regards the two longest objects on earth, which are the Great Wall of China and the line to the bathroom on St. Patrick's Day.

Credit: William Wade

Finally, there is one holiday that will get much more attention at the White House once I'm in office. And that, of course, is Mother's Day. Naturally, that is a day dear to my heart, and in honor of all you mothers out there, here is a poem I have written, entitled "An Ode to Mother," by Thelma Harper.

She was the one who carried you
until your first born day
and let you act as if
her sagging breast was a buffet.

You kept her up all hours
in your constant quest for food
and then your Daddy wondered
why she wasn't "in the mood."

While you were pinning tails
on a donkey for some fun
your Mama had the pleasure
of being married to one.

Later, she stood by you
like a lovin' Mama should
though she could have told you all along
your first spouse was no good.

So see your Mama often,
After all, you're next of kin.
And if picking her up is too much trouble,
She could always just MOVE IN!

Commonsense Answers from Your Candidate

THE QUESTION: Mama,
I plan to serve some
guests liver and onions
and brussels sprouts.
What should I follow
that with?

MY ANSWER: An apology.

Our Judicial System

As your candidate, I must address our judicial system, the legal profession, and the effects they have on our lives. First of all, we will always have a need for our courts. Our judicial system has been with us throughout history, going all the way back to the Garden of Eden, when Adam discovered a rib missing and came up with the idea of suing for personal injury.

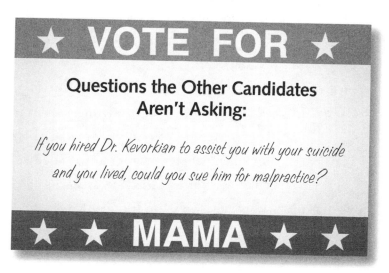

★ VOTE FOR ★

Questions the Other Candidates Aren't Asking:

If you hired Dr. Kevorkian to assist you with your suicide and you lived, could you sue him for malpractice?

★ ★ MAMA ★ ★

*My choice for chief justice of the Supreme Court. She's smart,
she likes bossing people around, and she already has a black robe.*

As citizens, we are all entitled to a fair trial, but there are too many loopholes in our judicial system that need to be examined. For example, the insanity defense is overused, and I think I will do away with it. Besides, I can tell you from personal experience: it's a waste of time on a parking ticket.

There are many courtroom tactics we should look at, including the most widely used defense strategy, which is lying to get acquitted. Most of our politicians started out serving the public as lawyers but sought greater fulfillment when they found that hoodwinking a jury of twelve people was not as satisfying as having a whole congressional district or state, and so, to this day, lawyers fill many of our institutions, like Congress, our local governments, and our minimum security prisons.

Even some of the most popular TV hosts are lawyers, like Geraldo Rivera and Tim Russert, not to mention that skinny gal who claims to be Star Jones, and, of course, Greta Van Cistern.

I am one of the few politicians who is not a lawyer, which ought to count for something. Still, I have a sharp mind and can sight many legal precedents as long as they were cases on *Law and Order*.

You may have gathered that I can be slightly negative about lawyers. Well, I'm not the only one. Over the years, I have heard many jokes that target attorneys. But as much as I might like to share some of those right now, this is not the right time or place to tell any of those jokes, like the one you may have heard that goes, "What do you call ten thousand lawyers at the bottom of the ocean?" "A good start." It's not right to tell jokes like that, and that goes for another one I heard, which begins, "How can you tell when a lawyer is lying?" "His lips are moving." Even other professions within our legal system are not immune from this type of cruel humor. Another joke you shouldn't tell goes like this: "What do you call a lawyer with an I.Q. of 75?" "Your Honor." I think you get my point, and I feel better now that I have reminded you to not share any of these jokes in public. By the way, I have many more I could warn you about if we're ever at a party together.

But here's the main problem with our judicial system: our courts are tied up with too many cases that take too long. They should take a hint from the TV court shows. On TV, justice is dispensed in thirty minutes, minus a commercial or two. If it's good enough for cases against auto mechanics and contractors, why not apply it to all the *other* criminals out there? When I'm president, I'll see that every citizen receives justice in front of a studio audience of their peers on one of our fine TV court programs. The one exception will be paternity cases, which will remain where they belong, on the Maury Povich show.

Morality in America

I have some views on morality I would like to share. Let me tell you what happened recently while I was traveling. I was in my hotel room, and a movie came on my TV. I think I pushed the wrong button. It was one of those movies you have to pay extra for. I thought it was going to be a love story . . . *Claudette and the Cable Guy*. But that wasn't cable he was laying. Take it from me . . . the Spice Channel has nothing to do with oregano.

Public morality is declining everywhere. You go to Disneyland and even Donald Duck isn't wearing any pants.

I have many thoughts on public morality, although some of my positions may surprise you. For example, my position on nude beaches. I actually have no problem with them. The way I see it, if God hadn't meant for some of us to go to the beach nude, he wouldn't have given the rest of us binoculars.

But I think we should do something about mothers nursing in public. Have you noticed how an ordinarily modest woman with a hungry baby turns into a Softee machine? Good Lord! Serve that lactating liquid lunch at home, in the car, or in the bathroom, but leave me out of it! Just the other day, I was at my favorite fine-dining establishment when some young gal whipped out one of her giant gazongas right in front of me. I was so disgusted, I almost upchucked my Grand Slam breakfast.

As you can tell, I'm for modesty and covering yourself up, but there's one exception. For women in all fifty states, I propose that public nudity be legal one day a year, in order to get your husband's attention during the Super Bowl.

Commonsense Answers
from Your Candidate

THE QUESTION: Do you
think it's good to talk
during sex?

MY ANSWER: Yes, but not
on the phone.

I will support the arts in America, even though a lot about the arts is confusing to me. And I'm not the only one. Take the world of fine art. Even the supposed experts often misspell the name of a famous painter, some spelling it M-o-n-e-t, and some spelling it M-a-n-e-t. But either way, the work he did on all those calendars and greeting cards is very nice, if you like flowers.

Yes, I will support the arts in America so that we can continue to have highbrow entertainment to put on public television to fill time in between segments of their pledge drive. And while we're on the subject, another thing that I've never understood is the ballet. In fact, a while back, I read a story about the English National Ballet. Apparently they banned several dancers from sunbathing because they weren't pale enough to play swans in *Swan Lake*. I'll tell you one thing: if ballet companies take things that literally, I wouldn't want to be a guy starring in *The Nutcracker*.

Another area of the arts that I don't understand is opera. You probably won't see any operas performed at my White House, although you're free to patronize the opera on your own time. Don't get me wrong. I have nothing against opera singers. They're certainly talented folks who can carry a tune. Let's just say many of them are among the people I suggested we ban from buffets, which I discussed earlier. The average opera singer is on the large side, and not just a little bit. Let's be honest. They're the sumo wrestlers of the music world. What are those opera singers eating and how often? Are they barbecuing backstage between numbers? You don't see fat singers in other types of music, except for that one guy, Ruben, who won on American Idol. And speaking of Ruben, I guess we shouldn't be surprised he likes to eat. He's named after a deli sandwich. I don't know what lies ahead for ole Ruben, but I think there may be an opera costume in his future.

★ VOTE FOR ★

Questions the Other Candidates Aren't Asking:

When I Love Lucy is dubbed in Spanish, does Ricky speak perfect English?

★ ★ MAMA ★ ★

Like many of our former presidents, I will support your right to enjoy oddball entertainment like the ballet and the opera. I'm actually kind of a musical gal myself, so don't be surprised if you're watching that PBS pledge drive one night and you hear the host tell Sarah Brightman to step aside and make room for "*Celtic Mama*".

Commonsense Answers
from Your Candidate

THE QUESTION: What isn't
over "till the fat lady
sings"?

MY ANSWER: An Aretha
Franklin concert.

As president, I intend to make it my business to shape up America's entertainment industry. I don't think those FCC people really know what they're doing. I've got bones to pick with reality TV, Hollywood, music stars, and celebrities.

REALITY TV SHOWS

I'll start with reality TV. I'm sick of all those reality TV shows, like *Survivor*. You know how *Survivor* works. They drop off a bunch of losers on some deserted island, and we're supposed to care. I'll tell you what I think. You want to put people somewhere where they won't stay around for very long, just stick them in President Bush's Cabinet!

And what is the story with Donald Trump? I'll tell you something: he doesn't need to hire a new apprentice. What he needs to do is find a good barber! What the devil is that wad on his forehead? I've pulled better looking hair out of my shower drain!

There are many shows on TV now about real estate and remodeling your house. Have you seen those shows where people show you how to decorate your home with junk purchased at flea markets? It's always the same. They buy the junk, bring it home, and paint it. I bought some junk and painted it. You know what I ended up with? Painted junk.

And what is the story with those cooking shows? Why is it, on every cooking show on TV, every time somebody tastes something, they go "Mmm . . . Mmmm . . . MMMM!"? Just once I'd like to see someone take a bite and say, "This tastes like crap!"

MUSIC STARS

We must have more supervision of our music acts, especially Britney Spears, who I will talk about in a minute. She's to parenting what Larry Flint is to good taste. Talk about a wild lifestyle. If Sodom and Gomorrah were around today, they'd name a street after her.

But she's not the only one who behaves badly. I read that a performer named Bobby Brown once dropped his pants and pointed his rear end at ten thousand people at a concert. I feel sorry for the fans holding up lighters. I was disappointed to hear that this young man mooned his audience. There's already enough crack at concerts.

CELEBRITIES

I thought you might like to know my opinion of some of the celebrities who fill the pages of our tabloids and magazines.

Paris Hilton

I'm glad Paris went to jail. That was for all of us who ever paid the Hilton three hundred bucks for a bed and a tiny bar of soap.

Did you all see Paris on *Larry King*? Good Lord! She makes Britney Spears sound like Eleanor Roosevelt. First it was Paris, and then Nicole Richie did some jail time. At least Nicole had a head start on the prison hunger strike.

Britney Spears

Now, there's a real piece of work. Do you remember when she had her head shaved? What would make a girl go into a hair salon and say, "Give me a Bruce Willis"? And y'all remember when she was on TV, kissing Madonna on the mouth? That was the most disgusting display of the tongue tango I've ever seen! I hope one of them had a cold sore. It would serve them right.

Madonna

You know, Madonna's writing children's books now. I believe she's released three children's books. I don't know . . . letting your children read a book by Madonna—isn't that a lot like putting Michael Jackson in charge of the Big Brothers of America?

Michael Jackson

And how about Michael Jackson? You know why he named his place the "Neverland Ranch," don't you? Because "Kinko's" was taken. Remember when he married Lisa Marie Presley? Even the llama was rolling its eyes. That marriage was doomed from the beginning. The way I heard it, when the minister said, "You may now kiss the bride," Michael said, "Do I have to?" What is his story, y'all? Before you could say, "Nutcase," he went from a young black man to a middle-aged white woman. You've seen his picture in all the magazines. He's the

Revlon cover girl from hell! And all those charges against him. I don't know about you, but I kind of wish he'd stayed with the chimp.

Tom Cruise

And what the hell has happened to Tom Cruise? That dumb cluck has gone crazy, hasn't he? I mean, you saw him on all the talk shows, acting like a baboon. I'll tell you what: he comes over to my house and starts jumpin' on the sofa, and he's gonna get his ass kicked! And he's on this whole anti-medication crusade. You know what I would love to do with that little shrimp? I would like to lock him in a room full of menopausal women. Nobody gets anything but a Centrum Silver, and we'll just see who comes out of there alive!

★ VOTE FOR ★

Questions the Other Candidates Aren't Asking:

If Elvis was such a big star, how come he's buried in his backyard?

★ ★ MAMA ★ ★

HOLLYWOOD

I have a lot of issues with Hollywood. For one thing, what's the story with all those Hollywood couples and their age differences? You've got Michael Douglas with Catherine Zeta-Jones, and Harrison Ford with that skinny little Calista Flockhart . . . you know, the actress from *Ally McBeagle*. If you ask me, Celine Dion started the whole thing, marrying that Canadian department-store Santa! Well, that's what he looks like. The last time I talked about those couples, someone said, "What about Demi Moore, who's over forty, with that young guy who's only around thirty?"

That, I see nothing wrong with.

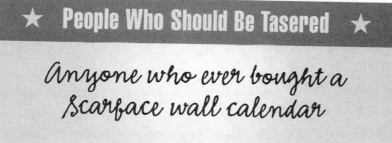

★ **People Who Should Be Tasered** ★

Anyone who ever bought a Scarface wall calendar

Why is Hollywood obsessed with dating shows, like *The Bachelor* and *The Bachelorette*? Whatever happened to meeting someone the old-fashioned way: in a bar, at closing time?

An interesting Hollywood fact for all of you: just like snowflakes, no two Burt Reynolds hairpieces are alike.

While we're on the subject of Hollywood, I want to take issue with *People* magazine's annual "Sexiest Man Alive" feature. I say, keep George Clooney and Brad Pitt. They're fine if you're thirty years old. I think it's about time they name a sexiest man alive for the rest of us. And I think the choice is pretty obvious. Here's his picture.

© Corbis

My nominee for People's *"Sexiest Man Alive":*
Mr. Wilford Brimley. He can test my blood anytime!

★ **People Who Should Be Tasered** ★

Entertainers who say, "Put your hands together,"
as if we don't know how applauding is done.

*L*et's talk about sports for a moment. First of all, I am as troubled as all of you about the use of performance-enhancing drugs by baseball players. My solution is to merge Major League Baseball with the World Wrestling Federation, and then it will no longer be an issue.

The amount of money paid to athletes is ridiculous. Take that MLB star Alex Rodriguez, who goes by the alias "A-Rod." He has a contract for $250 million! For that kind of money, a baseball player should come to your house and scratch his groin in person.

Professional sports are out of balance, and as president, I intend to do something about it. For one thing, there's too much violence in hockey and not enough in golf. I mean, you've all seen the fights that erupt on the ice. Just once I'd like to be watching a golf game and hear an announcer say, "Ladies and gentlemen, I can't believe it, but Phil Mickelson has his 4-iron wrapped around Tiger Woods's neck, and—oh my goodness—he's pummeling the young champion right there on the tenth hole!" Now, that would put a little much-needed excitement into golf.

On a nonpolitical note . . . ladies, here's something you might be interested in. I read an article that said you can determine a man's lovemaking ability by the sports he engages in. For example, a bodybuilder has size and power. A marathon runner has a lot of endurance. Needless to say, you should avoid a guy who likes miniature golf.

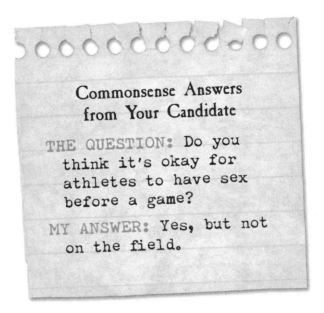

Commonsense Answers
from Your Candidate

THE QUESTION: Do you think it's okay for athletes to have sex before a game?

MY ANSWER: Yes, but not on the field.

It goes without saying that I will support our U.S. Olympic teams, but there are some things at the Olympics that confuse me. For one thing, it has come to my attention that the Olympics have been contemplating the addition of bowling. I don't know about you, but personally, I don't like the idea of a gold medalist who has to excuse himself to return his shoes.

A lot of you may not know this, but at the first Olympics, all the athletes were completely naked. It was there that a participant heard the seven worst words a nude relay runner can hear: "Sorry. I thought that was the baton."

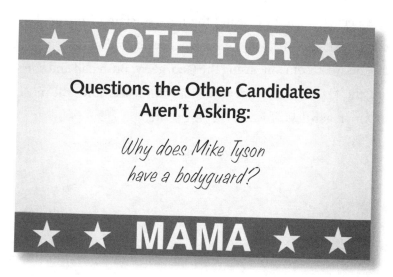

As you know, I mentioned the sport of bowling before. Actually, I think bowling is a fine activity that is not only fun but also rewarding, especially if you have a few bucks on the game. In fact, I have always wanted to own my own bowling alley. I hear the White House has a bowling alley. When I am president, I will give the White House bowling alley a makeover—it will have a unique political theme. As an educational and fun feature for the youngsters, all the bowling balls will commemorate former presidents and presidential candidates. Imagine how much fun it will be to stick three fingers into Jimmy Carter to pick up that seven pin on the left. Or how about sending Ronald Reagan to pick up a tricky 8-10 split on the right? And who knows what Bill Clinton will pick up! By the way, for the littlest tots, there will be a five pounder honoring former presidential candidate Michael Dukakis.

Even the pins will commemorate political figures, and, for historical accuracy, I will have the Gerald Ford pin specially designed so that it will occasionally fall down by itself. Finally, here's something

I'm especially proud of. Using the newest, state-of-the art bowling technology, all scores will be recorded electronically, so if there's a game between someone using the George W. Bush ball and someone using the Al Gore ball, whoever actually knocked down the most pins will win, regardless of who's keeping score.

*L*et's talk about getting around in this big country of ours. America is a nation on the move, and I intend to keep it that way. As a matter of fact, I do a lot of moving myself, and I'm not just talking about my restless leg problem. I'm talking about traveling. As the song goes, "I get around, round, get around, I get around." That's by the Beach Boys, the music group of the 1960s who popularized Hawaiian shirts even before there was a Timmy Bahama. By the way, the Beach Boys are still out there, but those rascals are about as old as I am, so the only surfing they do is probably for naughty pictures on the Internet.

But focusing on transportation . . . the condition of our roads and highways is very important for commerce, so it's logical that poorly maintained roads are bad for everyone. Well, I have a plan that will both maintain and beautify our highways. And here it is, America. This plan will require all of you to carry a shovel and some dirt in your cars. Then, while you're driving around, if you see roadkill along the highway, be kind enough to bury the poor little creature in a pothole and you will be killing two birds with one stone . . . or, in this case, one rodent with pile of dirt. I call this innovative plan my "Possum in the Pothole" program. However, do not get overeager and purposely aim for stray animals in order to participate. That was my "Kill It and Fill It" program, which never got past the planning stage.

As your chief executive, I will urge citizens to be more careful behind the wheels of their cars. I was out driving recently and saw a woman on the highway, doing 70 miles an hour, putting on her makeup! And she was weaving toward my lane. Stupid idiot! She scared me so bad, I dropped my phone into my coffee.

We must reduce the hostilities among motorists, even if the guy in the next lane is a moron. And we're all guilty of bad behavior. In case you were wondering who yells more obscenities at other drivers—men or women—actually it's equal, but women expect you to stop and listen till they're finished.

Mama for President

If James Bond had gotten his license to kill at the DMV, he would probably have used it before he left the building.

I will support our aerospace industry and those fine American companies like Lockheed Martin and Boeing. But you have to wonder about that British aircraft manufacturer, Airbus. That name doesn't aim too high, does it? If I'm going to be up in the air at 30,000 feet, traveling 400 miles an hour, I'd prefer not to be in a *bus*. If I want to travel by bus, I'll pack a bologna sandwich and go down to the Greyhound station, although I don't think I'd use the bathroom there.

And while we're on the subject of bathrooms, have you ever been in an airplane bathroom that didn't have a wet floor? It's a cesspool with the stupid metal toilet and waste receptacle overflowing and that construction paper passing for Kleenex. Because of what awaits me in there, I have been known to hold it from sea to shining sea.

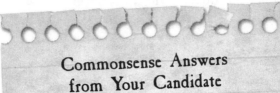

**Commonsense Answers
from Your Candidate**

THE QUESTION: Do you
have any advice for a
teenage girl with metal
braces on her teeth?

MY ANSWER: Yes. Don't
stand too close to the
refrigerator door.

Our Food Supply

*P*eople have asked what I will do to ensure the safety of our food supply, to prevent incidents such as recent recalls of spinach, lettuce, and beef. I have a lot of knowledge and experience on this subject. Over the years, I have been involved in the recall of many tainted foods. They were recalled right into my toilet bowl.

If you've ever had a bad stomach problem, you know that the Energizer Bunny isn't the only thing that keeps going and going and going. In order to prevent similar problems in the future, we need to step up our program to protect the nation's food supply. Well, my fellow Americans, I am not just your candidate; I am a foot soldier in the fight against indigestion.

It starts with cleanliness, whether it's

Mama for President

Never patronize a restaurant that offers "all you can keep down."

at home, at your neighborhood restaurant, or at a food processing plant. They can all learn a lot from me. My kitchen is more sterile than the operating room on *ER*. And here's another secret: I cook everything thoroughly. My eggs are boiled, my meat is broiled, and my prunes are as stewed as Willie Nelson on Saturday night. So rest easy, America. Once I'm your culinary commander-in-chief, you'll be in good hands. I'm proud to announce that for the protection of all Americans, I will soon propose a comprehensive new program of food safety guidelines that I call "No Intestine Left Behind."

And since I am a hands-on type, I will get involved right out there on the campaign trail, by staging surprise inspections at restaurants around America. So get ready, Mr. and Mrs. Restaurant Owner, because I propose to dive headfirst into restaurant safety and grab it by the meatballs.

★ **People Who Should Be Tasered** ★

Whoever's in charge of putting that one green orange in the bag of oranges at the supermarket.

And there's so much more to do. For example, I've heard a lot of reporting about new organic food regulations and the interest in organic foods. One voter asked me what the difference is between say, regular strawberries and "organic" strawberries. And the answer is, about a dollar a pound.

Here's an interesting food fact: guacamole, sloppy Joes, and chili all look the same after you eat them.

I was talking about prunes before. I hate when they change the names of foods we've gotten used to. For example, prunes are now officially known as "dried plums." Well, you can call them whatever you want, but whether it's "prunes" or "dried plums," take it from me: you'll be squeezing the Charmin after either one.

Credit: William Wade

When I'm president, I will exercise more control over fast food restaurants. For those of you who go to fast food restaurants, I have a question. What the devil is "popcorn chicken"? I tried it, and I still don't know. All I can tell you is it's definitely not popcorn, and I have serious doubts it's chicken.

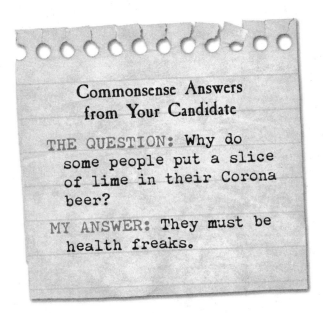

Commonsense Answers
from Your Candidate

THE QUESTION: Why do some people put a slice of lime in their Corona beer?

MY ANSWER: They must be health freaks.

Once I am president, I will abolish the food-runner system in restaurants. I can't stand it when someone takes your order and someone else brings you your food. How do I know the second guy isn't just a customer who didn't like the looks of that Salisbury steak and decided to dump it on *me*? Attention, America's waiters and waitresses: You took my order. You bring me my darn food!

Animals

I am your animal-friendly candidate because I believe it's good for us to have animals around. In fact, I read an interesting statistic I would like to share with you. I read that every time you walk a dog, there's a 25 percent chance you'll meet a friendly stranger. But be careful, because there's a 50 percent chance you'll ruin his shoes.

Dogs make wonderful companions. But have you noticed that they have the tendency to show up at the wrong time, like during a private moment. You'll be in the boudoir, trying to light a fire

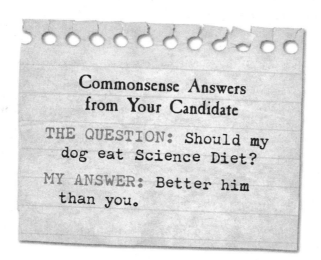

Commonsense Answers from Your Candidate

THE QUESTION: Should my dog eat Science Diet?

MY ANSWER: Better him than you.

under your spouse, and your dog will be right there, staring at you. Dogs like watching us in those private moments. It's their form of pornography. One time, just as my late husband and I were going to become intimate, I swear I saw our dog at the foot of the bed, eating popcorn.

A lot of people like cats, but they are a little too moody for me. You don't train cats. They train *you*. So I've never had a cat. And it was probably a good decision. I mean how much respect would I command in the world if foreign leaders knew I spent half the day on my hands and knees, coaxing a cat to come out from under the couch?

I will probably join many of our former presidents and have a pet at the White House, but I'm not sure what kind of animal to have. Maybe I'll have a dog, provided the vice president is willing to walk it. I know there is a risk that the dog would soil the White House Rose Garden when nature calls. But it can't be any worse than anything Billy Carter did out there. Of course, I will have my dog spayed or neutered to control his or her sex drive, which is something that might have been a good idea for some of our previous presidents themselves.

Maybe I won't get a dog. Why not give another animal a chance to win the international acclaim of being a pet at the White House? How about a parrot or canary or something like that? It might improve the image of our feathered friends since they have been so bad mouthed because of the Bird Flu. Wings and beaks may be the way to go, and as proof, imagine the history I'll make being photographed in front of the White House with the First *Duck*. Each morning, Cabinet members will arrive and greet me with a friendly, "Good Morning, Madame President. How's your bird?"

On the other hand, I might have goldfish. They are some of the most peaceful and beautiful of God's creatures, and if anything happens to them, it's all resolved with a simple flush.

We have many wonderful animals living here in America, and many of them are very talented creatures. For example, I have heard it said that dolphins are actually smarter than people. I suspect this might be true, and I offer as proof the fact that no one has ever seen a dolphin watch professional wrestling.

Chimps are also remarkably bright creatures. The only thing they can't understand is Bubbles's relationship with Michael Jackson.

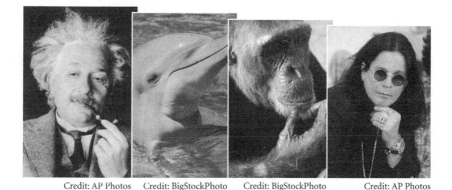

Credit: AP Photos   Credit: BigStockPhoto   Credit: BigStockPhoto   Credit: AP Photos

Mama's Intelligence Chart
(from the highest recorded intelligence to the lowest)

*F*amilies are the core of America. The fact that my family is a pain in the butt does not take away from that. So, since I'm running for president, I think it's only fair that I give you my opinions on family life. Raising children is difficult, especially when the little monsters misbehave. Just the other day someone asked, "Mama, what do you think of sending children to their rooms for punishment?" I love this question. Correct me if I'm wrong. In my day, you could punish the little curtain-climbers by sending them to their rooms. But nowadays, the average kid's room makes Chuck E. Cheese look like a detention center. Kids have their own TVs, radios, stereos, DVD players, and computers—complete with games and the Internet. If that's punishment, I'm Shania Twain. So I say, if you need to punish the little buttheads, punish away, but always stay on good terms with your kids because you never know when you may want to borrow their iPhone.

Let me tell you something that young couples do that irritates me. They'll say things like, "We just found out that we're pregnant." Don't you just love that? "We're pregnant." *We're* not pregnant. The woman is pregnant. The man got to have all the fun, and now he's going to stand around like a goon, holding his camcorder, waiting for the grand opening.

I have a proposal that is for the benefit of parents having a children's birthday party. It's very simple, and it will improve the quality of our lives. If the actor portraying Barney does more than one song, you don't have to pay him, and you can march his annoying purple butt right off your property.

Good family values come from communicating with your children. Sex education is an important part of that communication. Unfortunately, I wasn't that good at explaining the birds and bees. When my son asked me where he came from, I said, "That's what *we'd* like to know."

Women are having babies later and later in life—some well into their forties and beyond. In fact, I read about a sixty-three-year-old woman who had a baby. Her husband learned a real lesson: when you've had a condom in your wallet for forty-five years, don't expect it to work.

Birth control is important in order to limit our population growth. And there are many forms of birth control you can use. I will give you this advice: if your favorite form of birth control is the rhythm method, figure out the safe dates in advance. Never make love to your husband while trying to read a calendar stapled to the ceiling.

I am always studying and researching things in order to become a better informed candidate for you. In some of my recent research, I saw a study that says new parents can have relations right up to birth. Personally, I think once you're in the delivery room, you ought to just restrain yourself.

Commonsense Answers
from Your Candidate

THE QUESTION: Why is
it considered bad luck
for the groom to see
the bride before the
wedding?

MY ANSWER: Because he
might change his mind.

Everyday Annoyances I May Do Something About

*A*s president, I will have certain executive powers and privileges that I can use at my own discretion. I plan on taking full advantage of those powers to get rid of stupid things that annoy me. There are many things that irritate me, and I'm sure you're bothered by some of these things, too. For example, what the hell is a "certified pre-owned" Lexus? I'll tell you what it is. It's a damn used car! Get over it!

And why is there a tip jar at every take-out counter? Don't they know that avoiding a tip is the exact reason I'm taking out?

And when it comes to women's clothes, how the hell can there be a size "0"? If the size is 0, the price should be nothing, and you should be naked. Period. End of story.

Why does the supermarket cashier have to count all the cash

in her drawer after every darn transaction? Most people pay with a credit card. There's only three dollars in the cash drawer. Give it a break.

What's the story with non-Asian people who insist on using the chopsticks at a Chinese restaurant? Did you suddenly become Chinese when you went through the door? You know you can't eat with those things. Use your damn fork, and be proud you've mastered that. Besides, if going to a Chinese restaurant made you instantly Asian, we'd be sending our kids there to study for their finals.

We've all seen commercials on TV for music CDs. And there's nothing wrong with that. But my question is, how important is it for those CD music collections to offer rush delivery? I mean, how many people have to have *Bobby Vinton's Greatest Hits* tomorrow?

Sometimes I think our government agencies underestimate our intelligence. For instance, have you ever seen road signs near prisons that say, "Don't pick up hitchhikers"? What moron would pick up a guy in an orange jumpsuit, with a shaved head and lots of tattoos, not to mention the handcuffs and foot shackles? Like I'm really going to say, "Hop in, Baldy, and try not to scratch my upholstery with your shiv."

You want to hear something really stupid? You can now buy a machine to make s'mores . . . you know, that dessert with a graham cracker, marshmallow, and chocolate. What kind of idiot would buy a special machine to melt a marshmallow on a graham cracker? You already have the machine! It's called an oven! And furthermore, if you need a s'mores machine, you're eating way too many s'mores. Try having a piece of fruit. S'mores machines! No wonder so many of you are fat! Nothing personal.

Here's something that ticks me off: people who take more than five minutes to put cream and sugar in their coffee at Starbucks. First they study the different creamers like they've never seen them before. It's five minutes alone to decide on milk, low-fat milk, or half-and-half. And then there's the sweeteners. There's the white one, the brown one, the pink one, the blue one, and the yellow one. That's another five minutes. And of course, you've got to make sure you get the perfect wooden stick to stir with. And be sure to touch them all while you're at it. So they choose a stick and stir for a few minutes. Then they taste it. Now the whole process starts all over again—to mix a cup of coffee!! Good Lord! It took less time to create the polio vaccine! Put in some cream and sugar, and hit the road, moron!

Here's something else that bothers me at Starbucks. I went in there the other day and asked for a cup of coffee. The person behind the counter said, "Do you want me to leave room for cream?" When I'm paying a king's ransom for a cup of coffee, I want the cup filled so high they need a machine to wheel it to my table. The next time a coffee shop employee asks if you want room for cream, say, "Sure, and allow me to make sure there's plenty of room in your tip jar."

I'll tell you something else that irritates the devil out of me. You reach for your box of tissues to pull one out, and how many come out . . . about six, stuck together, right? Like we don't know they want us to buy that next box a little sooner. All I can say is, I'd like to blow my nose into the hand of the guy who came up with that little scheme.

And here's something we must put a stop to. At hotels, I can't stand it when the maid for my hotel room shapes the toilet paper into a

point. I've been traveling a lot and using a lot of hotel bathrooms. Now, in addition to hemorrhoids, I've got paper cuts on my butt. And do you know how hard it is to redo that point every time you

Credit: BigStockPhoto

finish in there? For crying out loud! Leave the toilet paper alone, or maybe roll the end up into a little ball or something, but no more points! By the way, I know I mentioned my hemorrhoids. It's okay. I'm an old woman. Some days, scratching those suckers is the only exercise I get. And that reminds me . . . I read that some people use that hemorrhoid remedy Preparation H to shrink the bags under their eyes. If it's true, I'd hate to find out where these people are squirting their Visine.

Mama's Campaign Cuisine

*Y*ou know, I have been in the kitchen most of my adult life, cooking dinner for my family. It's a hard habit to break. So you can rest assured that when I'm in the White House, I will be in charge of the cooking. Shoot, I might even reinstate Thomas Jefferson's famous "kitchen cabinet" because any mother can tell you that everything important in life gets discussed and probably settled in the kitchen. It is the heart of the home. You might be blue in the blue room, and bored in the board room, but the kitchen is always a happening place.

You can bet I'll be sneaking past those Secret Service boys to go to the kitchen for a little snack in the middle of the night, especially if some advisor wakes me up at three o'clock in the morning because he just has to have a response to some world crisis that can't wait till sunrise! It must be hard to get back to sleep when that happens. By the way, I hope they have an elevator at the White House because my old knees won't do those stairs so good any more. Anyway, I digress. I don't want all that fancy food at my White House, just good old, American, down-home cooking. And no diet food. Good Lord, nowadays everywhere you turn there's a new diet. Atkins-Shmatkins! No Weightwatchers, no South Beach, no North Beach, and no, I haven't called Jenny yet! I have always said: keep yourself moving, eat when you are hungry, and the rest should pretty well sort itself out. So with all this in mind, I have decided to share with America some of my all-time favorite recipes. If y'all are ever invited to one of my state dinners, you might get to sample one of these dishes, which are all part of the good food I'll be cookin' day one.

Credit: William Wade

MEATLOAF

Every woman needs to have a good meatloaf recipe in her repertoire. Most people think of Mom's meatloaf as dry and tasteless. How many times have you heard, "Good Lord, not meatloaf again!" In fact, a lot of people think meat loaf is the reason ketchup was invented. And that's because they don't have Jimmy Dean. He's not only a hunk, he's also a fine singer. Do you remember "Big Bad John"? I love that song.

Anyway, in 1969, he started making Jimmy Dean sausage, which is the secret ingredient in my meatloaf. Now, you are going to have to mix this up with your hands, so be sure you wash them first. And you'll notice that this makes a double batch. I always make an extra loaf because there's nothing better than a cold meatloaf sandwich the next day. This recipe is so good and easy to prepare, even my trashy daughter-in-law can whip it up and get rave reviews.

Mama's Meatloaf

21/2	pounds lean ground beef
1	log Jimmy Dean sausage (I prefer sage)
1	onion, chopped
1	cup saltine crackers, crushed
4	eggs, beaten
1	16-ounce can of tomato sauce
	salt and pepper to taste
	liberal sprinkle of Italian herbs (I probably use at least 2 tablespoons)

Mix together all ingredients with your hands. Shape mixture into two loaves. Grease two 5 x 9-inch baking pans and place loaves in pans. Bake at 350°F for 1 to 1¼ hours.

BEEF STEW

This is a hearty dish I'll bring over to my new neighbors in Washington when I go introduce myself. If they don't recognize me and ask which house I live in, I'll just tell them it's the big white one. Actually, I wonder who lives next to the White House. I hope they don't have loud parties. I'll need to get to bed early because, after all, I'll have a country to run.

Anyway, beef stew is a whole meal all in one pot, so it's perfect for a crowd. I might even serve it at a state dinner instead of that high-falutin' stuff with weird names like Rat-a-tooey, Fooey Grass, and Beef Borgnine.

Mama's Beef Stew

2–3	pounds beef chuck, cut in one-inch cubes
2	tablespoons shortening
2	teaspoons Worcestershire sauce
3	cloves garlic, chopped
1	large onion, sliced
1–2	bay leaves
2	teaspoons sugar
1	tablespoon paprika
1	tablespoon ground allspice or cloves
6	carrots, pared and quartered

1   pound of small white onions, peeled

6   stalks celery

2   tablespoons flour

     salt and pepper to taste

In Dutch oven, thoroughly brown meat in hot shortening, turning often. Drain fat. Add two cups hot water and the next nine ingredients. Cover; simmer for 1 1/2 hours, stirring occasionally. Remove bay leaves. Add vegetables. Cover and cook 30–45 minutes, or until vegetables are tender.

In a separate bowl, combine 1/4 cup water and flour until smooth. Stir slowly into stew. Cook and stir until bubbly, about three minutes.

CHINESE SALAD

I think food is a good way to improve foreign relations. Everybody feels more comfortable when they can get a little taste of home. So in an effort to welcome visitors from China, I'd probably serve my Chinese salad. But you don't need to be Chinese to enjoy it. It's an excellent dish for an emergency diplomatic summit or your church luncheon. I make most of it ahead and chill it. And then, when the Chinese ambassador shows up at the door, I'll pour him a tall frosty Tsing Tao (I think that's a beer), and then I'll run into the kitchen and finish the salad, so it'll be nice and crispy. You've heard of East meets West. Thanks to yours truly, now East *eats* West! (Try to say that three times fast!)

Chinese Salad

1	small can tuna
1	can French-style green beans
1	cup celery, finely diced
1	small can sliced water chestnuts
	dash garlic salt
11/2	teaspoons soy sauce
1	tablespoon fresh lemon juice
1/2	cup mayonnaise
1	small can chow mein noodles

Drain the can of tuna and can of French-style green beans. Mix together with the celery, sliced water chestnuts (drained), garlic salt, soy sauce, and fresh lemon juice. Stir in the mayonnaise. Chill for several hours. Just before serving toss, in the can of chow mein noodles.

BEER BUTT CHICKEN

Here's one of my personal favorites because it's not only delicious, it's fun to make. This will be the ticket when we have a big outdoor barbecue on the White House lawn. And it's as simple as can be. You don't need any fancy apparatus to make my Beer Butt Chicken. All you need is a couple cans of beer, a chicken, and a flair for proctology. If that's confusing, it will all become crystal clear when you read the recipe. Get ready for the compliments to come pouring in faster than you can say, "This bird's for you!"

Beer Butt Chicken

1	teaspoon paprika
2	teaspoons chili powder
1	teaspoon dried oregano
1	teaspoon salt
1	teaspoon black pepper
1/2	teaspoon cayenne pepper
1/2	teaspoon garlic powder
1	tablespoon packed brown sugar
2	12-ounce cans of beer
1	onion, coarsely chopped
2	cloves garlic, chopped

To make the marinade, combine the paprika, chili powder, oregano, salt, black pepper, cayenne pepper, garlic powder, and brown sugar in a bowl. Rub the marinade all over the chickens. Take the tops off two 12-ounce cans of beer and empty them about half way. Place 1/2 of the chopped onion in each beer can along with a clove of chopped garlic. Stand the chickens on the cans. Balance the cans on a medium-hot grill (indirect heat) for about 1 1/2 hours with the grill closed.

CHICKEN-AND-RICE CASSEROLE

There are a lot of middle-eastern dishes I just don't understand. For example, what's schwarma? What's tabouli? And who's Baba Ganoush? Sounds like the song Desi Arnaz used to sing. Well, apparently that's what they eat over there. I bet if I could get them some good, old-fashioned, stick-to-your-ribs American food, they might be in a better mood. Well, with that in mind, I offer my all-American chicken-and-rice casserole. It only takes five minutes to throw together, and ladies, while it's baking, you have time to throw yourself together for your husband. Bon Appetito! (With your dinner and with your husband!)

Chicken-and-Rice Casserole

2	cups white rice
4	cups water, divided
	whole fryer chicken, cut into pieces
2	cans cream of mushroom soup
	salt and pepper, to taste
1	envelope Lipton's onion soup

Place the white rice and 2 cups of water in a roasting pan. Lay the fryer chicken pieces on top. Mix 2 cans of cream of mushroom soup with the remaining water. Pour over the top of the chicken. Add salt and pepper to taste. Sprinkle with one envelope of Lipton's onion soup. Bake at 350 degrees for 1 1/2 hours covered, then 1/2 hour uncovered.

TURKEY MARINADE

Thanksgiving will be here before you know it. Will you be ready? You will now, thanks to me and my turkey marinade. And what's Thanksgiving without turkey? A great American named Ben Franklin wanted the turkey to be our national bird. Horsepuckey! The darn thing can't even fly. What kind of message does that send? Fortunately, he was overruled. Consequently, the eagle soars, and we can put the turkey in the oven where it belongs. So when I am president, I will feel no need to pardon a turkey on Thanksgiving. I'll be cooking one. And here's how.

Turkey Marinade

Makes enough for a 22- to 23- pound turkey

1	cup vegetable oil
1/2	teaspoon celery seed
1/2	teaspoon beau monde
2	teaspoons paprika
2	teaspoons dehydrated garlic (or 4 cloves of minced garlic)

To make the marinade, in a small bowl combine the vegetable oil, celery seed, beau monde, paprika, and garlic. Rub the marinade all over the turkey. Lift the breast skin and carefully put some marinade underneath the skin. For best flavor, marinate and refrigerate for 2 days before roasting. Follow standard instructions for roasting. (I like to roast my breast down until the last hour.)

TURKEY DRESSING

My turkey dressing is a work of art, although I wouldn't put it on the wall. It's a no-nonsense, all-inclusive dish. The great thing about it is that you don't have to make any potatoes because everything is in my dressing. And let's face it: it's all going to end up in the same place anyway. So go for it, and remember: a turkey without dressing is like a truck stop with no pork rinds. Dig in!

Turkey Dressing

Makes enough for a 22- to 23- pound turkey

8	large potatoes
12–14	slices torn bread
1	whole stalk celery, chopped
1	chopped onion
6	eggs, beaten
2–3	sticks butter, melted
1	quart whole milk
	Salt and pepper, to taste
	Poultry seasoning, to taste

Peel and boil 8 potatoes. When they are cool enough to handle, dice them and put them in a large mixing bowl. Add at least an equal amount of torn bread. (I use half wheat and half white, probably 12 to 14 slices of each.) Add most of chopped celery and chopped onion. Add 6 beaten eggs. Add 2 to 3 sticks of melted butter. Using a quart of whole milk, add enough milk to moisten the mixture. Mix thoroughly together with your hands. Add salt, pepper, and poultry seasoning to taste. Keep adding milk and mixing until it is really moist but not sloppy wet. Transfer the dressing into 2 small, greased loaf pans or 1 large casserole. Bake at 350° F uncovered for 1 hour or until golden brown.

CRANBERRIES

At Thanksgiving, I usually separate the grown-ups from the children. The grown-ups get to sit by themselves at one table, and we put all the little curtain-climbers at another one. Of course at my house, the maturity level is about the same at each table. But that aside, you can cover both of them at Thanksgiving with a cranberry sauce that the kids will love, and some sauced cranberries for the grownups. How sweet they are.

Kid's Cranberries

1	bag fresh cranberries
2	teaspoons sugar
1	15-ounce can crushed pineapple, drained
2	pints whipping cream
2	handfuls mini-marshmallows

In a blender, add the cranberries, sugar, and crushed pineapple. In a bowl, whip the 2 pints of whipping cream and fold in the cranberries. Fold in 2 large handfuls of mini-marshmallows.

Grown-Up Cranberries

2	bags of fresh cranberries
3	oranges peeled and quartered
11/2	cups sugar
11/2	ounces light rum
11/2	ounces Grand Marnier

Place all the ingredients in a Cuisinart, half at a time. Mince finely. Chill overnight; serve.

COUNTRY SPUDS

Everybody loves potatoes, but we are always looking for a new way to prepare them. Here is a great one because, after all, who doesn't love bacon? This is a little bit of heaven on your plate. My fellow Americans, you can take it from me. This is the side dish you've been dreaming of . . . except for those times that you dreamt you were naked and falling.

Country Spuds

1/2	pound thick sliced bacon
1 1/2	cups sliced onions
6	medium potatoes
	salt and pepper, to taste
1 1/2	cups whole milk
1/4	cup parsley, chopped

Cut the bacon crosswise into 1/2 inch pieces. Sauté the bacon until crisp. Remove the bacon and drain on paper towels. Sauté the onions in the bacon drippings until tender. Set aside 1/2 of the onions. Cut the unpeeled potatoes into 1/4-inch slices and arrange 1/2 of the potatoes over the onions in the skillet. Sprinkle the potatoes with salt and pepper. Add the remaining onions, top with the remaining potatoes, and sprinkle again with salt and pepper. Carefully pour the milk over the potatoes. Add the bacon and heat to boiling. Reduce the heat and simmer covered for 25 minutes or until the potatoes are tender. Sprinkle with remaining bacon and parsley.

HOLIDAY DIP

What's a get-together without a good appetizer? That's where my holiday dip comes in. I'll probably serve this to soften up some foreign leaders who need a little attitude adjustment. I'll have them eating out of the palm of my hand, although I'd prefer they use a plate. This will be what each trusted ally and global partner will see first when they walk in for our friendly White House holiday open house . . . after they've been thoroughly frisked, of course. And then, let the festivities begin, starting with a tasty treat that would do any party proud, as long as everyone knows that there will be no diplomatic immunity when it comes to double dipping.

Christmas Dip

2	pounds hamburger meat
1	cup onions, finely chopped
1	large can tomato sauce
1	large can pork and beans
	salt and pepper, to taste
	chopped olives (optional)
	tortilla chips

In a large skillet, sauté the hamburger meat with the chopped onions. Add the can of tomato sauce and the can of pork and beans.

Add salt and pepper to taste. Simmer slightly. If desired, sprinkle with chopped olives. Serve warm with tortilla chips.

CHERRY WINKS

Here are some festive cookies that are fun for the kids to help with. And they're rolled in corn flakes, so I guess they're kind of a health food dish. You know, cherries are a wonderful little fruit hand-picked in Oregon, which happens to be the maraschino cherry capitol of the world. I don't believe there is actually a maraschino cherry tree. I think instead, the cherries are just well preserved, kind of like me. By the way, I don't want to neglect my constituents in Michigan—they also grow a lot of cherries. Try using red or green cherries, or both, depending on the holiday. And let's not forget the connection to our first president, George Washington, who cut down the cherry tree and then escaped across the Potomac standing up in a boat.

Cherry Winks

21/4	cups flour
2	teaspoon baking powder
1/2	teaspoon salt
3/4	cup softened butter
1	cup sugar
2	eggs
2	teaspoons milk
1	teaspoon vanilla
1	cup chopped nuts

1   cup dates, finely cut and pitted

1/3   cup maraschino cherries, finely chopped

3   cups corn flakes, crushed

     maraschino cherry halves

In a medium bowl, stir the flour, baking powder, and salt together. Set aside. With a large mixer beat the butter and sugar until light and fluffy. Add the eggs; beat well. Stir in the milk and vanilla. Add the flour mixture; mix well. Stir in the nuts, dates, and chopped cherries. Shape the dough into tablespoon-sized balls and roll them in the crushed corn flakes. Place the balls on a greased baking sheet and press a cherry half into the center of each ball with your thumb. Bake at 350° F for 10 to 14 minutes until light brown.

Alright, no more beating around the Bushes—our government has spent itself into a financial mess! The party's over, people! America's VISA card has hit its credit limit. We've got bills we can't pay, and Social Security is on the brink of going bankrupt! I'm not saying it's time to start selling off our historical monuments on eBay . . . yet. But we do have to do something to raise money to pay off this ridiculous bazillion dollar debt!

I promise if I am elected president, one of the first things I'm going to do is ask Congress to enact some new taxes. Now, before you go getting your panties in a wad, hear me out on this. You just might agree with some of my new taxes.

First, I think there should be a "showing a fifty-year-old belly button in public" tax. I'm sorry, but some things need to remain covered—potato salad at a Fourth of July picnic, manholes, and a fifty-year-old belly button. A fifty-year-old belly button should know its place. It's too old to be playing peek-a-boo. I don't care if it's an outie or an innie, at fifty it's time it grew up. And don't even get me started on belly button rings! Why in the world would a fifty-year-old woman get a belly button ring? To hang her car keys from so she won't forget where she put them?

Another tax that I would propose would be a Speedo tax. (This might need to be passed into law.) I'm not sure who invented Speedos, but, like diapers, Speedos should come with a pound limit. Just like you can't find Pampers in the 70- to 90-pound range, you shouldn't be able to find Speedos in the over-250-pound range. And here's another thing. Who decided that grown women should wear overalls? We need to put a tax on that. You either need to be under five years of age or you need to have Uma Thurman's body. Otherwise, no overalls, Sweetcheeks. Talk about doing our part to keep America beautiful!

I will also be proposing a "bad comb-over" tax. Let's face it, this tax should have been enacted years ago. There have been far too many people getting away with this ridiculous deception for far too long. By my calculations, the "bad comb-over" tax will go a long way towards paying down our national debt. Why, the money we raise from televangelists alone could fund our entire national defense budget!

Other taxes that I plan to propose to Congress are:

The "telemarketer calling during supper" tax

The "two shopping carts and 57 coupons in the express lane" tax

The "crying baby on a crowded airplane" tax

The "quit tailgating me, you moron!" tax

The "never hanging up your cell phone even when you are next to me. I do not want to hear your life story" tax

The "celebrity Bimbo gone wild" tax

The "dress caught in the back of your pantyhose" tax

The "idiot parking so close that you can't get into your car" tax

The "teenage heavy metal band practicing next door" tax

The "weighing the same at your twenty-year reunion as you did in high school" tax. (This, too, might need to be made into law.)

I have plenty more taxes to propose. But you can see where I'm going with this. None of us would mind paying taxes if they were just the right kind of taxes!

More Ways to Pay off Our Nation's Debt

*M*y new taxes should go a long way toward paying off the national debt. But that's not my only idea for raising or saving money. I have others. One especially innovative idea of mine is to start offering glamour photos at the DMV. If you're one of the few who actually enjoys carrying around a picture of yourself looking like you haven't slept for eight days, just got word from your doctor that you might not make it through next Tuesday, and the toxins in your system are making your skin break out in some sort of strange lesions—the likes of which haven't been seen since the last bubonic plague outbreak—then this part of my platform probably won't interest you. But if you're like the rest of us, a glamour photo for your driver's license sounds like an idea whose time has come. And one that most of us wouldn't mind paying a little extra for.

Let's face it, most DMV workers have extra time on their hands in between ignoring the people standing in line and ignoring the phones that are ringing in the background. I think they could squeeze in a wash and set every once in a while. And since they're already dealing with the fingerprint inkpad, how much more stress would a makeup kit add?

They should also offer different backgrounds for our driver's license photos, like they do at Wal-Mart. These would be for a nominal surcharge, of course. But people would pay it. After all, a cop would have to be a heartless cad to still give you a ticket after you hand him your driver's license with a picture of you in a field of daisies.

Speaking of police work, I would recommend offering glamour mug shots for celebrities, too. Do you think Nick Nolte wanted a picture of himself in the news with his hair looking like he went through a car wash the hard way—without a car? Of course not! Had someone offered him a glamour mug shot instead of the finger-in-the-socket pose that he got, I'm sure he would have signed up for it in a heartbeat. Who knows, even Scarface Capone might have turned his life around if he hadn't been so depressed over his mug shot. But with a little cover up over the scar, a nice skin exfoliate, and a new haircut, he might have been a model citizen.

And what about that astronaut gal—the one who drove nine hundred miles from Houston to Florida wearing her Depends? I'm sure she would have gladly paid for a makeover before that awful mug shot of her was broadcast all over nationwide television. By the way, if you're going to be in the news for chasing down your boyfriend's new girlfriend, that's not the picture to endear people to you, much less make your boyfriend want to come back.

Another way I plan on raising money is to triple the cost of a postage stamp. Now before the national whining begins, listen to my reasoning on this. When you consider a letter can spend three months going between planes, trains, and mail trucks, traveling all the way from Los Angeles to Des Moines to Orlando to New York and then back to its original destination, anything under two bucks is still a bargain. Besides, they keep raising the price of stamps by two cents every other month so that you have a drawer full of useless stamps. I say, let's bite the bullet, America, and do it all at once and that will save us from having to buy those dang two cent stamps to go along with our leftovers that don't work anymore.

I'm not only about raising money, I'm also about saving money too. For instance, I say let's get the Jehovah's Witnesses to also take our national census. They're already going from door to door.

I'm sure I'll come up with more deficit-busting ideas, but for now that should convince you that I am the candidate who will once and for all get us in the black. Red's never been my color anyway.

More Deficit Busting

*H*ere is one more proposal for busting the deficit. Do you have any idea how many geniuses we have living right here in the good ol' US of A? I'm not talking a 4.0 grade average, college-scholarship type. I'm talking about all of our off-the-chart geniuses; the people whose IQs astound you, like what about that cute little fellow that was on Jeopardy, Ken Jennings; what about Stephen Hawkings; what about Bill O'Reilly, oh never mind, he's just a smart ass; but you see where I'm going with this. Why aren't we doing more to take advantage of these people's collective brain power?

Let's have a national "Pay It Forward" television tournament. I say we round them all up and put them on game shows like *Jeopardy*, *Who Wants to Be a Millionaire*, and *Wheel of Fortune*. We'll make it their national responsibility—kind of like jury duty. All the money they win in the game will be put toward reducing the deficit, and you know they will play their hearts out because who wants to look like a moron in front of 60 million people?

The whole country would be cheering them on. I'm not sure

how many weeks they would have to play to reach a trillion dollars, but I'm sure they could get it done within the time frame of my administration.

Here's another great idea. I'm not much of a gambler myself, although I do play the penny slots now and again, and I did wear a plaid dress once that my family said was a bit of a gamble, but I think I have found the proverbial lifeboat coming for us and I say, "Let's jump in it." It's time for the United States to open its own casino. If the Indians have it figured it out, why hasn't the government? If it's not legal yet in Washington DC, we will just stick a riverboat out on the Potomac. You know what they say, the house never loses, and even if it does, you know how much the government is going to take out of your winnings in taxes. I tell you, we are looking at millions of dollars coming into the treasury. And we will be happy to serve you a free cocktail, from a big-busted government employee while you are losing your shirt on behalf of America.

Another way that we could raise much-needed funds is to follow the lead of the Girl Scouts. How much money do you figure they raise each year by selling their cookies? It has to be in the millions. So why isn't the government following this same fund-raising technique? Let's get Ralph Nader on board. He's always whining, so let's put him in front of a Kroger with a table full of cookies and a sign that says, "Do-Si-Dos for the Deficit" or "Samoas for the Shortage" or my personal favorite, "Thin Mints for a Thinning Economy"?

We aren't using our heads, people. We all know we have a huge problem. So let's quit complaining about it and start doing something about it! These are all good, solid ideas. But I can't do it alone. The people of America have to help me out a little. If you have some innovative ideas for raising money to help pay off the deficit, e-mail me at:

Thelmaharper@quityourbellyachinganddosomethingaboutit.com

I promise that every cent I don't use for my campaign will go directly towards paying off the deficit.

My Presidential Limousine

*D*on't get me wrong. The presidential limousine is nice and all, but if I'm elected president I would make a few changes. For one thing, I don't think we've ever had one with its left turn signal permanently stuck in the "On" position, but it's an added security measure that's long overdue. Think about it. What better way to keep would-be assassins off guard than by having the presidential limousine always signaling for a left turn, but never actually turning? They wouldn't know what to think. I'm surprised the Secret Service hasn't thought of this already.

For years people have scoffed at us elderly drivers who forget our turn signal is on. But we haven't forgotten. We know good and well it's on. We just don't give a horse's patoot. We're doing it for our own protection. Why, do you have any idea how many follow-home robberies take place against the elderly each year? We can't fight them all off with our purses, you know! If we can throw off just one assailant and keep him from following us home and trying to do us harm, then leave us alone and let us flicker away to our heart's content!

Another thing that I will have added to my presidential limousine is a hot tub . . . unless, of course, Bill Clinton already had one installed. A hot tub is just the thing that a president needs after a hard day of dodging the press. Toss a couple of cups of Epsom salt into the water, have the driver put on a Vince Gill tune, and, well, you get my drift.

The limousine could probably use a luggage rack, too. A presidential limousine should be able to hold the jumbo-sized model. That would come in handy when we go to the airport to pick up the Queen. I don't know how they've been picking her up before, but I'm sure she'd appreciate the extra luggage space just for all her hats.

I don't want to say anything out of line, Lord knows I always try to be tactful, but I think the presidential limousine could really use a, well, you know, a "facility." The presidential motorcade can't just go pulling into a Texaco, you know. The whole place would go nuts! *"Say, isn't that the leader of the free world over there buying a Big Hunk bar?"* It would cause total chaos, but what else are you supposed to do? If you need to stop, you need to stop. And in my case, I sometimes need to stop a lot. Shoot, I'd never make it through the Inaugural Parade without at least three or four pit stops. But if the presidential limousine had an onboard "facility," then this type of embarrassing situation would never happen. It would also reduce the risk of Madame President walking out of a filling station dragging a train of toilet paper behind her. All our enemies would need is to get their hands on a photo like that and hold it for ransom.

Finally, with as many photo ops as the presidential limousine gets on a regular basis, it seems to me that we're missing a great marketing opportunity here. Do you realize there isn't a single bumper sticker on the presidential limousine? Not one. We could fix half the potholes in America with the money we could raise if we'd just start selling advertising space on the First Car! Imagine it—the next time the presidential motorcade rolls through your town, you'd see bumper stickers with familiar-sounding product slogans. I envision the presidential motorcade looking like a NASCAR automobile. We could be sponsored by Earl Schieb and Jiffy Lube. We could even have a giant bumper sticker saying *Goodrich Tires Are Protecting Her Butt*. If you think about it, this could mean big advertising bucks for our country. And that's just the rear bumper! We'd have the whole rest of the car to fill up!

Mama's Famous
Women Quiz

_H_ ere's a little test of your knowledge about famous women. We political gals have said some pretty profound things. Can you match the lady with her quote? Let's find out. If you get more than half right you're a genuine feminist. If you get less than three right, it's time to pound down some estrogen and get in touch with your feminine side.

WOMEN LEADERS

_____ 1. Hillary Clinton

_____ 2. Margaret Thatcher

_____ 3. Indira Gandhi

_____ 4. Imelda Marcos

_____ 5. Madeleine Albright

_____ 6. Condoleeza Rice

_____ 7. Ann Richards

_____ 8. Geraldine Ferraro

_____ 9. Princess Diana

_____ 10. Margaret Dole

_____ 11. Eleanor Roosevelt

_____ 12. Queen Elizabeth II

_____ 13. Nancy Pelosi

_____ 14. Dianne Feinstein

_____ 15. Barbara Bush

_____ 16. Thelma Harper

QUOTES*

A. "Win or lose, we all go shopping after the election."

B. "We need a common enemy to unite us."

C. "You don't have to have fought in a war to love peace."

D. "If I want to knock a story off the front page, I just change my hairstyle."

E. "You cannot shake hands with a clenched fist."

F. "Let me tell you, sisters, seeing dried egg on a plate in the morning is a lot dirtier than anything I've had to deal with in politics."

G. "If you want something said, ask a man…If you want something done, ask a woman."

H. "Nobody can make you feel inferior without your consent."

I. "America must be a light to the world, not just a missile."

J. "It's all to do with the training. You can do a lot if you're properly trained."

K. "You have to learn the rules of the game. And then you have to play it better than anyone else."

L. "The only way to keep from going crazy in this house is to stay half lit."

M. "We have learned that power is a positive force if it is used for positive purposes."

N. "People think that at the end of the day a man is the only answer. Actually, a fulfilling job is better for me."

O. "To understand Europe you have to be a genius—or French."

P. "I married the first man I ever kissed. When I tell this to my children they just about throw up."

Key: 1–D, 2–G, 3–E, 4–A, 5–O, 6–B, 7–F, 8–C, 9–N, 10–M, 11–H, 12–J, 13–I, 14–K, 15–P, 16–L

*All quotes taken from thinkexist.com, famousquotes.me.uk, about. com:womenshistory, and imdb.com.

*E*veryone knows the president must be well dressed. Well, I thought you might have a little fun dressing me! On the following pages is a paper doll dummy of me and some outfits I'm considering wearing as your next president. For a sneak preview of what's in store for the American public, dress me up!

Credit: William Wade

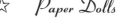

Credit: William Wade

Credit: William Wade

Credit: William Wade

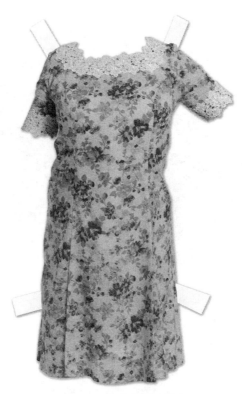

Credit: William Wade

Credit: William Wade

Credit: William Wade

Some Thoughts on Relationships

I believe every American has the right to a healthy relationship, but one per person, please. And I don't want to know what you're doing. I believe intimacy is a personal matter best left to the privacy of your own car.

As for me having a relationship at the White House, I'll be flying solo. So don't look for any First Gentleman accompanying me. At

Commonsense Answers
from Your Candidate

THE QUESTION: Mama, how can I get my husband to take more time with me during lovemaking?

MY ANSWER: Try gluing the TV remote to your stomach.

my age, finding a mate is not worth the aggravation. Not that I didn't try. But I gave up awhile back when eHarmony.com forwarded my application to the AARP.

On the positive side, my having no relationship, or even no desire for one, will eliminate the possibility of a scandal during my presidency. Yes, America, you can breathe easy because once I inhabit the Oval Office, the only thing under my desk will be some varicose veins and a pair of sensible shoes with odor-eaters in them.

But rest assured that I will be the candidate who's not afraid to discuss the intimate facts of life. For example, I am not against sensuality between lovers and even being creative in that area, as long as you know what you're doing. For example, eating off of your lover's stomach is romantic, if it's something like strawberries. Never eat a pot roast that way.

I have many opinions on the subject of sensuality. For example, people have asked me "Mama, do you think it's okay for a woman to take nude photos for her husband?" I say yes, as long as it's not in that little booth at the mall.

One priority of my presidency will be to try to instill more elegance and respectability into our citizens, especially the young men out there. I have a lot of advice and guidance for you. For instance, if you're a young man shopping for your girlfriend at Victoria's Secret, have some class. Don't ask to be directed to "the cheapest underpants that show stuff."

And here's a tip for elderly ladies. Boxer shorts decorated for Valentine's Day are okay, but leave it at that. Don't draw hearts on your husband's Depends.

Commonsense Answers
from Your Candidate

THE QUESTION: Mama, I need your advice. My husband and I haven't been intimate for a year, and frankly, it's because he weighs 350 pounds. He keeps asking me what's wrong, and I've tried to be nice about it, but the other day I told him why I'm not interested, and he was crushed. What should I do?

MY ANSWER: You better leave well enough alone. With your husband at 350 pounds, if you do become intimate with him, he's not the only one who'll be crushed.

My Inauguration

*M*y inauguration will be a day to remember! Everyone will be all fired up, and our capital will be buzzing about the new gal in town! Of course, as cold as Washington DC gets in January, I almost wish I was still going through menopause. Talk about a good way to keep warm—one of my hot flashes once set off a smoke alarm!

As one of my first priorities, I will acknowledge my loyal constituency of senior citizens, so after I'm sworn in on the Bible, I'll be sworn in again on a copy of *Readers Digest*.

And then, I'll show the world what a forward-thinking individual I am and connect with the young people out there by delivering the first U.S. inaugural address done in the form of a rap. It'll go something like this:

> **Whassup, my name is Thelma,**
> **and I'm here to say,**
> **If you really wanted a change,**
> **it's your lucky day.**

You men stop wonderin',
no need to speculate,
I measure 44-36-48.

Show me some respect,
don't forget I paid my dues,
or I'll kick you in the butt
with my sensible shoes.

Don't mess with me,
or you know where you can go.
I'm as mean and nasty
as your HMO.

I haven't picked out my ball gown yet, but I'm sure I'll find something simple but elegant, and hopefully as uplifting as my speech will be. You see, I don't just need support at the polls, if you catch my drift. But I'm sure I'll find something nice. Penny's usually has a good clearance sale around September.

Maybe Barbara Bush will let me borrow one of her dresses and some of her pearls, provided those are real. In fact, I can actually see myself becoming best friends with Babs. We're both outspoken gals with a lot of mileage on us, and we can talk for hours about how mixed up our sons get. Not only that, but she and I would agree that if you are going to hang around the Oval Office, it works out better if you are a little oval, like we are. Apparently, that other woman who's been running for president this year knows that too. Thank God for pants suits in plus sizes, right Hill?

Even though my son irritates the heck out of me, I will get him a good seat at the inauguration because, about a year ago, he predicted I would be elected. Well, he didn't actually predict it as you might think. His exact words were "Mama, you'll be president the day a woman with one leg goes on *Dancing with the Stars.*

Speaking of dancing, I will attend every inaugural ball in my honor. I've seen "W" dance, and I know I can cut a rug every bit as good as he can. Matter of fact, if running the country doesn't take too much of my time, I might just go on *Dancing with the Stars* myself. I can dance rings around Marie Osmond and remain conscious after I do it.

After the swearing in, my riveting specch, and the inaugural balls, I'll officially move into the White House. Good Lord, I hope the Bushes hire good movers and will have gotten all their stuff out of there by then. I'm an old woman—tripping over cowboy boots in the middle of the night could be fatal. Here's my policy on moving in: if you left it behind, it goes on the curb. Case closed.

Well, I'm bound to be pretty tired by the end of the festivities. Once the night is over, I'll put all the leftover inaugural food in Tupperware to lock in the freshness. I'll give those containers a good burp, have a good one myself, and turn in for the night. God bless America!

My Presidential Library

After a term or two as president, each chief executive gets a place to stash things they have no space for in their garage. That place is called a *presidential library*, although you can't borrow books and there's no newspaper on a big stick. Instead, they are like museums where you can go and get a glimpse into the lives of the inspirational individuals who possessed enough character, principles, and integrity to claw their way to the White House.

I am proud to announce that after I finish the U.S. presidency, all of my memorabilia will be stored at the Thelma Harper Presidential Library. And what an enlightening center of knowledge and history it will be. In addition to boxes of my check stubs and old receipts, there will be a gift shop, café, and a Bingo room.

I'm sure Americans will enjoy spending time at my library reflecting on my administration and all of my accomplishments, if there are any. You'll be welcome to come in to relax, reflect, and cough up a few bucks for knickknacks and souvenirs. For your safety, all souvenirs manufactured in China will be separated into two sections: leaded and unleaded. And I'm proud to announce that my presidential library will be the only one with a gift shop offering the full line of Dr. Scholls products, including their very effective corn remover.

As with other presidential libraries, many of the gifts I receive from foreign leaders will be on display, unless they were personal items like a nightgown, corset, or other undergarment. I hope you understand.

In addition to things collected while in office, I'm proud to announce that some of my most treasured possessions will be on display at the library. Just to whet your appetite, let me say that if you like admiring fine things, you'll love looking at my commemorative plates. My favorites are the ones depicting the Oak Ridge Boys. They look pretty realistic, or at least as realistic as you can look on a plate. I have each Oak Ridge Boy except the weird-looking one with the long beard.

And since I believe fine art is for everyone, at the Thelma Harper Presidential Library, you will be able to buy some of the beautiful paint-by-number artwork I did for my women's group fund-raisers. I will also be selling a s'mores machine I received as a Christmas gift from my son last year.

My Final Remarks

*A*nd now you have read what I have to offer as a presidential candidate. I hope we will meet somewhere on the campaign trail so I can pass some time with you. (Why not? At my age, time is about the only thing I can pass without any difficulty.) And it is my fervent wish that you all will gang up and elect me as your president and then have the pleasure of watching as I assume the position. I'm running to give America a boost. And you obviously need a boost. Why else would so many of you buy the Wonderbra, padded panties, and push-up jeans?

But let me end my message on a profound note. We need to go back to when America enjoyed peace and prosperity. Join me, and together we will set America back.

Thanking you in advance, I am—still—Thelma Harper.

* * * * * * * * * * *

Well, look at you: you got to the last page.
I sure as hell hope you bought this book by now,
for crying out loud!

* * * * * * * * * * *

Acknowledgments

*I*t was a little less than one year ago that I started laughing about this idea and thinking it would be a funny book. Mel Berger, my literary agent at William Morris, made it happen rather quickly by book standards, and, along with him, there is a number of people whom I need to thank for that. Sandy and David Brokaw have been my publicists and friends for years now. I want to thank them for making this book a reality—most especially David for his personal involvement in the whole process. He is an avid fan of politics, so his hours of mentoring for this project have been greatly appreciated.

Monty Aidem and I have been writing together for a long time. We worked together before I even had my talk show. He's an LA guy from San Fernando Valley, and he is the antithesis of Mama, so it has been an interesting journey helping him learn to speak in Mama's vernacular. He's gotten exceptionally good at it, and I thank him for all his hard work on this project.

A huge thank you to all of the good folks at Thomas Nelson. They've been so patient and so helpful. Pamela Clements, my publisher, is, as far as I can tell, the main reason you are holding this book in your hands. She has been a cheerleader, a psychologist, a sounding board, a tough disciplinarian, and ultimately a new best friend. At the very least, I owe her a huge debt of gratitude and probably a Calgon bath as well! Additional thanks go to my editor Emily Prather, typesetter Walt Petrie, and editor-in-chief Geoff Stone. Finally, thanks are owed to Renee Reed for her help in acquiring and creating the hilarious photos in the book.

As always, thank you, thank you, and thank you to Carol Burnett. Mama was created for her, but Carol wanted to play Eunice and wanted me to play Mama. So I have often said that Mama is yet another gift from Carol. I love her with all my heart.

Finally, there would be no reason for this book without my exceptional fans. Honestly, Mama has had a much better career than I have! When I perform, my audiences range from ten to ninety years of age, and for that I am so grateful.

Last, thank you to my husband and my best friend, Al, for his endless support and encouragement. He reads the paper to me in the morning while I am stretching, and we brainstorm funny new ideas together. I would be lost without his enthusiasm. I know it is Al's nightmare that one morning he will wake up, roll over, and be lying next to Mama. I hope that never happens . . . but I do know that if it does, she'll make him laugh!